DEPRESSION
A Cognitive Approach

DEPRESSION
A Cognitive Approach

Geoff Tomlinson
& Dawn Slater

www.speechmark.net

First published in 2003 by

Speechmark Publishing Ltd, Sunningdale House, 43 Caldecotte Lake Drive, Milton Keynes MK7 8LF, United Kingdom
Tel: +44 (0)1908 277177   Fax: +44 (0)1908 278297
www.speechmark.net

Reprinted 2010, 2013

002-5119/Printed in the United Kingdom by CMP (uk) Ltd

British Library Cataloguing in Publication Data
Tomlinson, Geoff
   Depression : a cognitive approach. – (A Speechmark practical therapy manual)
   1. Depression, Mental – Treatment   2. Cognitive therapy
   I. Title   II. Slater, Dawn
   616.8'527'0651

ISBN 978 0 86388 403 0

Contents

contents

HANDOUTS

Introduction

Who can use this book?

Depression: A Cognitive Approach is designed for professionals to use when working with clients who are suffering from depression. Any mental health professional or support staff who are supervised, and who have some knowledge of psychological interventions, can use it. It is based on cognitive behaviour therapy. A detailed knowledge of cognitive behaviour therapy is not essential, but some familiarity with this mode of treatment would be helpful. The manual will give detailed instructions on how to proceed, starting with identifying the patient's profile of depression, through to identifying dysfunctional thinking patterns and then looking at ways of overcoming these.

The experience of depressive symptoms can range from the mild and temporary lowering of mood and negative thoughts that most people experience when an unpleasant event occurs, to that of a very severe depressive illness that seriously disables the individual. It is easy to recognise the difference between these two extremes — for example, when a relationship breaks up it is normal for a person to be tearful, sad and experience feelings of low self-esteem. If this person still experiences these feelings in a year's time, this may be considered an abnormal reaction. However, most people with depressive symptoms fall somewhere in between these extremes.

Treating someone with a severe depressive illness should only be done by an experienced therapist, and even they may require help from other professionals such as a psychiatrist or a community psychiatric nurse. As most people with depressive symptoms fall in the middle of the range, the therapist should ensure that the client is properly assessed. This may be aided by the use of rating scales such as the Beck's Depression Inventory (Beck *et al* 1961) and the Hamilton Rating Scale (Hamilton 1960) alongside their normal clinical assessment. This book can be used by staff who are relatively inexperienced in treating depression. However, when this is the case they should receive regular, appropriate supervision.

Who will benefit?

The methods described can be used with people who are suffering from most types of depression. They can be used with clients with mild to moderate depression in most therapeutic situations, and with people suffering from severe depression if they are in an in-patient setting. They are most effective with people with mild to moderate depression, as the people with whom they are used need to have some motivation. People who are so severely depressed that they are extremely withdrawn, or who are also experiencing psychotic symptoms, would need to be in-patients.

Sometimes depression is a reaction to other mental or physical health problems. While this manual will not necessarily help overcome these problems, it can still be used to help with the depressive problems that are complicating the other illness. Cognitive behaviour therapy has been shown to be effective in the management of most psychiatric disorders (Dobson 1989; Hollon & Najavitis 1998), and has also been shown to be effective as an adjunct to the treatment of some physical conditions.

Cognitive therapy can also be used to work with people in a group setting. For this purpose it is recommended that groups have six to eight members to allow each individual to receive the benefits. Too few and the dynamic aspects of the group can be lost, whereas too many can prevent the exploration of the individual's problems. When used in a group setting it can be helpful to have a mixture of people with both mild and moderate depressions. This is because the less depressed often appear positive to the more depressed, and can act as a reminder of how they were. In contrast, the more severely depressed allow the less depressed individuals to see that things are not as bad as they may perceive them to be. As progress in the group is only as quick as the slowest member, the range of severity should not be too great. Despite this, group members will progress at different rates, and this should be expected. You should normally expect the group to run for between 20 and 25 sessions. The last sessions may be spaced further apart, as in individual treatment. The spacing out of sessions helps the client to gain more confidence in managing their depression.

Outline of the book

The book is divided into three parts: Part 1: Basic information
Part 2: Therapeutic steps
Part 3: Additional information

Part 1
This will cover the main body of the information that you will need. It will consist of:
- Principles of cognitive therapy
- The cognitive model of depression
- Using cognitive behaviour therapy with depressed individuals
- Reasons for failure in cognitive behaviour therapy
- Combining cognitive behaviour therapy with other approaches
- Other models of depression

Part 2

This consists of a series of steps in the treatment of depression. It contains most of the practical guidance that you need to help someone overcome depression. It consists of 10 steps:

Step 1

This concerns the identification of the client's depressive symptoms, and helping the client to recognise their own particular symptom profile.

Step 2

This concentrates on the causes of depression, identifying various models in general, and describing the cognitive behavioural model of depression in detail. It is important that the client understands this, as it will be the treatment approach described.

Step 3

This focuses on identifying the client's level of activity, and ways that their activity can be increased. In the cognitive behavioural model it is often necessary to start with the behavioural elements before being able to proceed to the client's cognitive difficulties.

Step 4

This describes the nature of negative automatic thoughts, and will enable the therapist to teach the client how to recognise their negative automatic thoughts.

Step 5

This focuses on being able to exert quick control of negative automatic thoughts. These are usually used at the beginning of therapy, in order to help the client get some sense of control of their symptoms.

Step 6

This deals with ways of challenging negative automatic thoughts. These are seen as being fundamental in generating the client's depressed mood. Therefore ways of overcoming them are essential in helping the client to feel better.

Step 7

This looks at behavioural experiments. Behavioural experiments are ways in which negative automatic thoughts that are not open to direct cognitive challenge are dealt with in the cognitive behavioural framework. They consist of identifying abnormal beliefs that the client has, and then setting up experiments that the client can test out in between sessions. The client is instructed to use the knowledge they have gained to help them identify and change any abnormal thinking patterns.

Step 8

In this step, the client is taught how to challenge assumptions. In the cognitive behavioural model, the development of dysfunctional assumptions in earlier life is what led to the client's vulnerability to depression. By this stage in therapy, the client and the therapist should have sufficient evidence to identify and subsequently challenge dysfunctional assumptions.

Step 9

This step describes problem-solving. Problem-solving is fundamentally a cognitive behavioural approach and therefore fits well with cognitive behavioural therapy.

Step 10

This helps you prepare the client for discharge, and looks at relapse planning. It is anticipated that clients may have relapses in the future, and ways of identifying these and 'nipping them in the bud' are discussed. This step also involves trying to identify periods that may be stressors in the future, so that the client can prepare for these and minimise their effects.

It is expected that some of the steps may require a longer time-scale than others. This is negotiated between the therapist and the client, to provide a structural framework that both can follow, but which can be modified to address individual needs. For example, it may take three sessions to complete Step 2. The emphasis is on successful completion and understanding for the client. There may also be occasions when therapist and client need to return to a step to allow the client to get back on track (for example, they may have expressed difficulties since the last session). This is common when challenging negative automatic thoughts and dysfunctional assumptions.

Part 3

The third and final part of the book covers other aspects of depression, and other additional information needed to help the individual. There are three main sections to this part.

Section 1

This begins with a description of drug treatments in depression, and describes methods to increase the adherence to medication and the awareness of the effects of medication.

Section 2

This describes how to manage suicidal ideas and thoughts of self-harm.

Section 3

This deals with special groups suffering from depression. These include bipolar disorder, seasonal affective disorder, and postnatal depression.

The nature of the therapeutic relationship

The emphasis is placed on the quality of the relationship between the client and the therapist. They should take an equal and active responsibility while working through the book. This involves the establishment of a collaborative relationship between therapist and client. In order for the relationship to be effective, both must have trust in each other, and honesty in their interactions and feedback.

Although they have different parts to play, their goal should be the same – that is, for the client to understand their depression, and to have the ability to identify the factors that may contribute to it, and the role that their cognitions play in the maintenance of their depression. The client should be guided towards exploring and identifying alternative methods of coping with aspects of their lives that they find difficult. This is not always possible without help. The therapist's role is to encourage the client to understand these difficulties. They may be easy for the therapist to identify, but it is for the client to recognise them and want to explore the choices they may present. The therapist should support the client in this exploration by providing objective and defined feedback, as well as guidance in understanding and overcoming their dysfunctional thinking patterns. It is for the therapist to enable the client to discover the answers.

It may be beneficial for the therapist to let the client know that therapists are human, and that while they may have never experienced depression, they have experienced the difficulties that life invariably gives us.

What needs to be known about the client before the treatment begins?

Prior to beginning therapy with the client, you should have knowledge of their social, physical and psychological history and, in particular, areas of risk relating to the client. As the cognitive model is essentially a developmental model, it is important to take a life history.

This will help in understanding the way the person thinks about themselves and their world. You may learn about significant events in the client's life that have influenced their belief systems. The therapist should be aware of any medication that the patient is taking, and if they are also receiving therapy from someone else.

What the client needs to know about the therapy

The client needs to understand the difficult climb they have ahead, and that some aspects of this journey may be painful and will require emotional and physical effort. They need to feel that they have support and understanding during this time.

They need to understand the basic approach to therapy, and be prepared to attend regular sessions. They need to be committed to the whole treatment, which is usually 12 to 20 sessions, which would normally last for 1 hour (1 ½ hours in groups) at weekly intervals. For in-patients, the sessions may need to be shorter and more frequent — for example, for 20 minutes three to four times a week. The reduced length of the session is because in-patients may find it difficult to concentrate for the full hour. In-patients will usually be more severely depressed, and will gain more from more frequent sessions as the gains made in each session are more likely to be maintained if the time between each session is reduced.

Sometimes clients will withdraw from therapy. This should be negotiated with the client if possible, and the reasons why they wish to withdraw should be explored. The opportunity to return to therapy should usually be offered. Prescribed medication, rest and physical care all contribute to recovery, and can be used in conjunction with the methods described in this book.

The client will experience good and bad days, and recovery may be gradual. The therapist should identify these periods and ensure that the client is aware of the normality of this pattern.

Basic Information

Part 1

Principles of Cognitive Therapy

Introduction

Cognitive therapy is usually a short-term treatment in which the therapist tries to help the client to develop more effective methods of dealing with troublesome thoughts, feelings and behaviours. It is a problem-orientated approach that addresses the difficulties people face in their day-to-day life that have provoked their depressive symptoms. It also works on the underlying cognitive difficulties related to the development of their depression.

Cognitive therapy, like other psychotherapeutic approaches, needs the application of both empathy and understanding. The therapist is more active than in psychodynamically orientated psychotherapy or client-centred approaches. The therapeutic relationship in cognitive therapy is described as being one of collaborative empiricism (Beck *et al* 1979). By this it is meant that both therapist and client are expected to take an equal and active responsibility. The therapeutic approach is empirical as it collects evidence and tests the client's beliefs.

The therapeutic relationship is developed by:

- Socratic dialogue
- Giving and receiving feedback
- Setting and reviewing homework

The therapist takes responsibility for establishing the therapeutic alliance, and assumes the therapist takes the role of expert in understanding cognitions. The client is seen as the expert concerning knowledge about themselves. This idea of shared expertise should be conveyed to the client to build up the collaborative nature of the relationship.

Developing the therapeutic relationship

Socratic dialogue

One of the main ways of developing the collaborative relationship is the use of so-called Socratic questioning. This refers to a style in which the therapist asks questions in order to help the client to understand their difficulties. Therefore, the therapist will ask questions rather than provide solutions, even if they know one. In this way, the patient finds the answers to the questions, and this proves more effective than answering questions for them. The method itself can be quite time-consuming, but the results are worth the effort. For example, in the exchange detailed below see how the therapist encourages the client to follow the chain of their cognitions back to the underlying beliefs that they have concerning their own incompetence.

CLIENT	I have been feeling miserable all week.
THERAPIST	Can you tell me about this?
CLIENT	Well, it just seems to have been there all the time.
THERAPIST	Can you say when it began?
CLIENT	It just seemed to be there all the time.
THERAPIST	What about last weekend?
CLIENT	Well, Saturday and Sunday weren't too bad. My husband and I went out together to see friends.
THERAPIST	So it must have begun after the weekend?
CLIENT	Well, I suppose so, but I remember at work feeling miserable, although when I first went to work on Monday morning I wasn't too bad.
THERAPIST	What happened on Monday morning?
CLIENT	My boss was in a bad mood and was going on about not being able to find some papers that he wanted.
THERAPIST	What was going through your mind at that time?
CLIENT	I thought that the boss was blaming me for the problem and that he was probably thinking that I am useless.
THERAPIST	You were thinking that the boss thought you were useless?
CLIENT	Yes, that's right.
THERAPIST	I remember you saying that your boss is often like that.
CLIENT	Yes, he's like that with everyone.
THERAPIST	Was he like that with other people that day?
CLIENT	Yes, he was in a bad mood with everyone that day.
THERAPIST	So let's review what we have just covered. You started to feel bad on Monday morning. And this was following you thinking that the boss was criticising you. However, it sounds like the boss was just being his normal self. After you felt criticised you started to feel miserable, is that right?

As you can see, the therapist posed many questions. The therapist may have been aware of the relationship between the client and her boss, and could probably have said to her at the very beginning that he thought that the depressed mood was associated with this situation. However, by getting the client to develop the story she is able to see the links for herself, and this is more effective.

Giving and receiving feedback

Another way of developing the collaborative relationship is the giving and receiving of feedback. From time to time, the therapist will ask the client for feedback about what they have been told or discovered during the session, and for their understanding of this. The therapist will also give the client feedback at regular intervals. This could take the form of a summary of what has gone on in an exchange between them. In the example above there is a short summary of what the therapist believes the client said.

Setting and reviewing homework

Just as the therapist is quite active in the sessions, it is important that the client also demonstrates high levels of activity, especially in between the therapeutic sessions. To some extent, this is achieved by the setting of homework assignments or other self-help activities. The use of homework tasks in between sessions is fundamental to cognitive therapy, and is seen as a way of broadening and generalising its effects. The skilled therapist must be able to set relevant and focused homework tasks to enable the client to work on their difficulties. To reinforce the importance of homework, it should always be reviewed in the next session.

How cognitive behaviour therapy is delivered

A typical course of cognitive therapy for depression lasts between 12 and 20 sessions. Each session normally lasts for one hour and occurs initially at weekly intervals. Towards the end of therapy, the sessions are usually spaced out to every two weeks and then every four weeks. Sometimes a 'booster' session is planned for two or three months after the end of the course to review progress and sort out any difficulties the client is having in using the skills acquired during the therapy.

For hospital in-patients, the frequency of the sessions could be up to three times per week, and the number of sessions required could well be higher due to the severity of the patient's symptoms. Also it may be difficult for severely depressed patients to concentrate for one-hour sessions, so it may be necessary to have the sessions for shorter periods. (Beck *et al* 1979; Wright & Beck 1983; Bowers 1990; Thase & Wright 1991.) As the patient recovers they will probably be discharged, and then therapy would usually proceed as described above for out-patients.

When cognitive therapy is being delivered to groups, the sessions should last for one-and-a-half hours. The groups normally have between six and eight people in them; more than eight could make it difficult for all the clients to discuss their problems. The group usually lasts for between 20 and 25 sessions.

The Cognitive Model of Depression

Introduction

The cognitive model of depression mirrors the cognitive model of other psychopathologies. It emphasises the centrality of negative thinking styles in producing the depressed mood. The cognitive model is a holistic model that recognises the importance of biological, psychological and social factors. The negative thinking styles that are seen as central to the generation of abnormal mood states are believed to have developed from earlier life experiences, and therefore the cognitive model is essentially a developmental model.

The cognitive model is based on the concept that our reactions and emotions to events are mediated by our thoughts. This means that what we think about events, rather than the events *per se*, determine, how we respond both behaviourally and emotionally. How we process information is not fully understood, but it is clear that the brain is able to process and respond to incoming information rapidly and in a complex manner. We have developed ways of ordering information to enable us to respond quickly to incoming information. Ordering information enables the brain to link incoming stimuli to past events and this leads to the development of beliefs or rules about the world and our place in it. When a belief is generated, it exerts a significant effect on the way incoming information is processed. The earlier a belief is developed, the more fundamental or core it is. It is also less sophisticated and therefore tends to be less flexible and more pervasive. Our beliefs change throughout our lives. Earlier beliefs may change completely, but they may also remain unchanged. Change is more likely if the belief is not associated with a lot of negative emotion.

Very young children do not have the capacity to differentiate things as well as older children, and therefore beliefs generated at this time will be pervasive and unconditional, allowing for no exceptions. Early information-processing and belief generation may occur in the preverbal phase of development, in which case beliefs may not be easily expressed in words, but be experienced in emotional or bodily sensations. A young child learns that hot things burn and cause pain. This may be learnt by direct experience of touching something hot, or by verbal instructions from a parent. These rules tend to be absolute, and therefore have no exceptions. These develop into core beliefs. The core belief that hot things burn and are painful is one that most of us share. However, we also develop other core beliefs that are more idiosyncratic. These develop from personal experiences – for example, if a very young child repeatedly experiences violence associated with the return home of an intoxicated parent, then they may develop a belief that all drunk people are aggressive. If this belief develops in a preverbal phase, then the child might become very anxious whenever they smell alcohol. They may not be able to explain why this is, despite later developing a more sophisticated understanding of the effects of alcohol on people, as they never significantly changed their non-verbal core belief.

Later learning is more sophisticated and allows for variations in the rules. A very young child might have been frightened by a dog, and therefore developed a core belief that dogs are frightening. This core belief may persist into adulthood. If, however, a child encounters a dog for the first time when they are somewhat older, they may be able to recognise that some dogs bite and are best avoided, but that some dogs are friendly and can be a source of fun. The child might be able to further elaborate this rule by describing how to tell a friendly dog from a dog best avoided. These sorts of rules are not absolute and there are exceptions. In cognitive behaviour therapy these kinds of rules are called dysfunctional assumptions if they are unhelpful. The older a child is, the more sophisticated is their thinking, and the more elaborate are the rules that they generate to help in their decision-making processes. However, as noted earlier, the child's new beliefs are built upon the earlier core beliefs, and these may not be easy to change if they are suffused with emotion. This pattern of thought is common to us all and describes how both helpful and unhelpful beliefs develop.

Information-processing is still more complex than this description, as not all the information that is received is attended to, and even the information that is received is not all given the same level of importance. The brain has ways of selecting what is attended to. This process of selecting information is affected by our existing beliefs. Information that is in line with our beliefs is more likely to be accepted than that which contradicts it.

The model suggests that people with depression have developed core beliefs or assumptions about their world or themselves that are inaccurate and unhelpful. However, the client may well be unaware of the inaccuracy of their beliefs. To them, their beliefs seem self-evident. Their dysfunctional assumptions may well remain dormant for long periods until they are activated by some event. When core beliefs or dysfunctional assumptions are activated, they generate negative automatic thoughts. It is the experience of negative automatic thoughts that leads to the depressed mood and affects the person's behaviour. The person's mood and behaviour can also lead to the generation of more negative automatic thoughts, as they usually lead to further activation of the dysfunctional assumption or core belief. This is why the depressed mood persists even if the activating event has ended. This model of depression is represented in Figure 1.

Negative automatic thoughts

The term 'automatic thoughts' is essentially synonymous with self-statements, private thoughts, or internal dialogue. They tend to occur without any deliberation, and unless challenged tend to be accepted without question. Automatic thoughts are part of normal everyday life, but within conditions such as depression and other psychiatric problems they

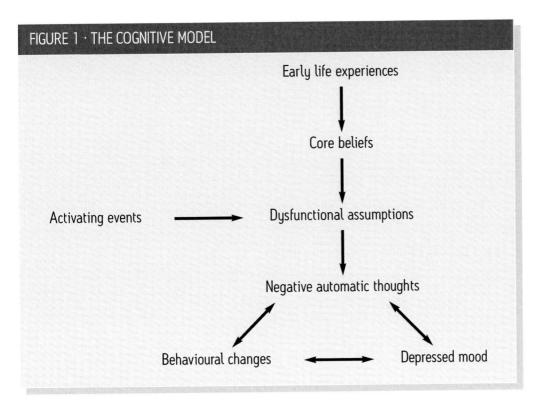

FIGURE 1 · THE COGNITIVE MODEL

tend to have a repetitive, and dysfunctional content (Beck 1976). They interact with mood states to amplify the level of emotional distress. Research has shown that there is a high correlation between measures of automatic thoughts, dysfunctional attitudes and ratings of symptomatic severity. This suggests that cognitions have a prime role in the development of mood disturbance (Beck 1976; Clarke 1986; Shaw & Segal 1988). Some people can recognise their automatic thoughts without difficulty, but others find it hard to recognise their thoughts, especially during the early stages of therapy. Part of the role of the therapist is to help the client to learn to identify their negative automatic thoughts.

The content of negative automatic thoughts usually corresponds to the perceived meaning of the event that precipitated the emotional upset. Automatic thoughts can be triggered by memories, daydreams, and anticipated or hypothetical events, as well as by external events. Because the content and frequency of negative automatic thoughts are correlated to the level of mood disturbance, it would be reasonable to accept the mood disturbance as a justified reaction to the negative automatic thoughts if they were an accurate reflection of reality. This means that anyone who had a high frequency of negative thoughts would expect to feel depressed. The abnormality in depression is the inaccuracy or distortion of the client's thoughts.

Negative automatic thoughts are often associated with errors in information-processing, as summarised in Table 1, page 10. Identifying and demonstrating these cognitive errors provides one of the tools for intervening therapeutically. There are 10 thinking errors that are common in negative automatic thoughts in depressed people. Although non-depressed people may also have the thinking, they are not as extreme or as frequent.

TABLE 1 · COMMON THINKING ERRORS (SEE HANDOUT 2 FOR STEP 4)
1 · All-or-nothing thinking
2 · Over-generalisation
3 · Mental filter
4 · Disqualifying the positive
5 · Jumping to conclusions
6 · Magnification or minimisation
7 · Emotional reasoning
8 · Shoulds, oughts and musts
9 · Labelling and mislabelling
10 · Personalisation

By analysing the content of a series of automatic thoughts, it is possible to infer a deeper cognitive structure. It is the patterns of negative automatic thoughts that lead to the identification of dysfunctional assumptions and core beliefs. These dysfunctional assumptions and core beliefs are not always in conscious awareness, but are usually easily accessible through the techniques used in cognitive therapy, especially Socratic questioning.

Dysfunctional assumptions

These are beliefs that order our thinking. They are commonly laid down in childhood, and are formed either as a result of repetitive life-experiences or, occasionally, a single traumatic experience. As the most important sources of experience in childhood are our family, beliefs and attitudes can be passed on from one generation to the next. Dysfunctional assumptions sometimes appear to be the same as commonly held beliefs; however they tend to differ in their intensity or extremeness. Therefore, they may not be perceived as problematic, and may even lead to traits that are seen as desirable, especially by others. For example, being conscientious is usually accepted as a good attribute; however, if it is held to an extreme it may lead to the individual feeling overwhelmed by all the things that they are expected to do, and lead to a sense of failure. Most people have exceptions to their rules. So, in the case of conscientiousness, most people are able to accept that at times their own needs may mean that they have to do a job to a satisfactory level rather than the very best that they can. The person who has a dysfunctional assumption associated with conscientiousness will not be able to compromise in this way.

Dysfunctional assumptions are conditional in nature. This means that they are activated only in certain conditions, and lie dormant when the conditions are not present. Dysfunctional assumptions often have an 'if ... then ...' structure. For example, 'If I am not successful then no one will like me', or 'If I'm criticised then it means that I'm a failure'. This means that it is possible to escape the effects of the assumption. In the first example, it is clear that if the person remains successful, then they will feel liked or wanted. However, if they become unsuccessful – say by being made redundant, or by failing an examination – then the belief would be activated. The redundancy or failing the examination acts as the activating event. The person then begins to feel that they are a failure, and this in turn leads to feeling that they will be disliked, and the consequences of that will be that they will be alone, and this makes them feel depressed. Most people would feel depressed if they believed they were going to be disliked and alone (Figure 2).

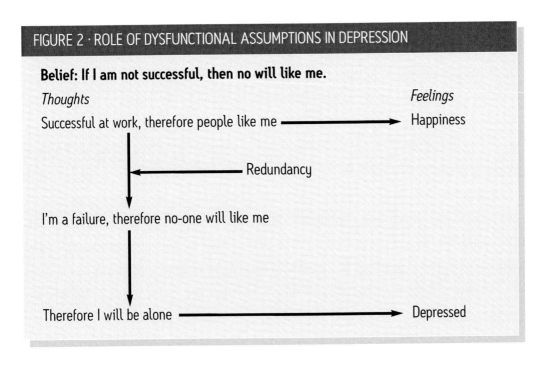

FIGURE 2 · ROLE OF DYSFUNCTIONAL ASSUMPTIONS IN DEPRESSION

Belief: If I am not successful, then no will like me.

Thoughts   *Feelings*

Successful at work, therefore people like me ⟶ Happiness

⟵ Redundancy

I'm a failure, therefore no-one will like me

Therefore I will be alone ⟶ Depressed

In depression, the dysfunctional assumptions are generally about loss of either social contacts or social standing, and are often associated with self-criticism and low self-esteem. Table 2 shows several examples of common dysfunctional assumptions.

TABLE 2 · EXAMPLES OF DYSFUNCTIONAL ASSUMPTIONS

1 · In order to be happy I have to be successful in everything I do.

2 · To be happy I have to be approved of by everyone I meet.

3 · If I make a mistake I am a complete failure.

4 · I cannot be happy without a close relationship.

5 · If somebody disagrees with me, it means that they do not like me.

6 · I am only worthwhile if others think that I am.

Core beliefs

Core beliefs can be conceptualised as enduring patterns that serve as our basic, yet unspoken, rules of life. As mentioned earlier, they are shaped through interactions with the environment and, although they may evolve over time, they tend to be laid down in the early part of life. They serve as summaries of principles that permit memories and recollections of multiple experiences to be stored and organised according to single themes and rules.

Core beliefs tend to be expressed in absolute terms – for example, 'I'm bad,' 'I'm incompetent'. As they are pervasive, they tend to affect all areas of a person's thinking. In order for the core belief to remain intact, the brain has to selectively attend to or ignore incoming sensory information. Anything that is incongruous with the core belief is ignored or distorted. So, if someone who has a core belief about being bad is given some positive feedback, for example 'helping me get that job done was really useful', they are likely to say to themselves something like: 'they're only saying that to humour me, or so that I don't get annoyed'. This explains why any data that is inconsistent with the core belief is not attended to.

Negative information, however, is readily attended to, and is interpreted in line with the core belief. The following example demonstrates how negative feedback is accepted without criticism, and the positive is distorted:

Bob, who believes that he is a failure, is due for his appraisal. His appraisal is generally favourable, but there are a few criticisms of one or two aspects of his work. Bob leaves the appraisal feeling very depressed. He says to himself that he always fails at everything. Even the things that went well were so simple that no one could get them wrong, and anyway he didn't do them as well as other people.

The core belief exerts an influence every time a subject to which it refers is raised. As the core belief is so embedded in the person's thinking style, it tends to be accepted without question. When the therapist points out the core belief, the client is often surprised to find that anyone could consider it abnormal. They may even think that everyone else has a similar belief.

The cognitive model therefore proposes a structural hierarchy of cognitive processes in which negative automatic thoughts are seen as the end point of a sequence deriving from core belief and dysfunctional assumptions.

Introduction

Cognitive behaviour therapy focuses on the current patterns of the client's thinking. Therefore, the problems that the therapy focuses on are mainly in the here and now, and are of current concern.

The therapy is very transparent in that either the rationale for any intervention should be obvious, or the therapist should be able to give a rational explanation for the intervention to the client. To this end, any 'jargon' should be kept to a minimum. The therapist should always try to use everyday words, and if the client has their own idiosyncratic words or ways of describing things then these should be used when possible.

Therapy begins by explaining to the client the therapeutic style of cognitive behaviour therapy as being one of collaborative empiricism. Collaborative empiricism is characterised by the therapist and client both taking active roles in the therapy and working in conjunction with each other to solve the problem. This should be explained to the client. The empirical approach is based on the scientific method of testing the evidence against the hypotheses. The sessions will be structured as described below. This basic structure should be adhered to as much as possible. The structure of the sessions mirrors the approach to dealing with the client's depression.

Structure of the session

The typical session will consist of the following:

1	Setting the agenda	5 to 10 minutes
2	Reviewing the homework from the previous session`	5 to 10 minutes
3	This week's task	30 to 40 minutes
4	Setting homework	5 to 10 minutes
5	Reviewing the session and feedback	5 to 10 minutes

Agenda-setting

Setting the agenda for the session usually takes between 5 and 10 minutes. This can often be a difficult task, especially if the client has lots of things they want to tackle. They sometimes want to put too many things on the agenda. Although the client usually chooses the agenda items, the therapist must help the client to choose the most effective topics for the agenda. At the beginning of therapy, the therapist should try to guide the client towards easy topics that will lead to quick and successful outcomes. This means trying to focus on small problems which, although they may not be of great importance for the client to resolve, will almost certainly lead to a successful outcome. This can sometimes be achieved by breaking down a problem that the client brings into smaller bits. The rationale for this approach is that it is better to succeed in a small task than to fail at a larger one. Success leads to an improvement in the client's level of depression, even if only temporarily. At the beginning of therapy, the client needs to learn various skills, and these need to be built into the sessions' agendas. These skills are described in the various steps in this book.

Later on in therapy, the bigger and more fundamental problems can be tackled. By this time, the client will have become more proficient at using the techniques they will have learnt during the therapy.

Time must also be left for review of the previous week's homework; setting homework for the current session, and review of the session.

Reviewing the homework from the previous session

It is important to do this every week. If it is not reviewed, the relevance of doing it can be lost. Most of the therapeutic gains are achieved through the homework. This is because the things that are learnt in the session are put into practice in real life, and the relevance and effectiveness of the therapeutic interventions are best realised in this way.

First check that the homework was done, and how the client got on with it. Did they have any difficulty? Is there anything from the homework that they want to talk about? Did it trigger off anything else that they think is relevant?

If everything went well, then move on to the next topic on the agenda. However, if things went wrong then it may be necessary to negotiate a change in the agenda in order to discuss the difficulties that the client had. The therapist must decide on the importance of the problems with which the client had difficulty. If the problems are connected with a lack of understanding of the nature of the therapy or cognitive model, then they will probably lead to difficulties in sessions to come, or in future homework. Therefore, at some stage they will have to be resolved.

If the problem is not fundamental, it is probably better just to note the difficulties for future reference so that they can be dealt with either in future sessions or homework. This decision should be conveyed to the client.

This week's task

This will form the main part of most sessions. Each topic normally takes between 10 and 20 minutes to tackle. Therefore, two to three things can usually be tackled in a session. Sometimes a problem is clearly going to take longer, and if this the case then up to 40 minutes can be allocated, but only one topic would then be covered. If, during the session, it becomes apparent that the problem is going to take longer than expected, then it will be necessary to discuss this briefly with the client, and to decide whether to carry on with the topic and adjust the agenda, or to leave the topic unfinished and return to it at a later date.

The content of the topics usually comes from events that have occurred recently, or from the homework, and therefore there is normally no difficulty in finding topics. At the beginning of therapy the topics will generally be about current symptoms and behavioural difficulties that the client is having – for example, problems with motivation; not being able to cope, or negative thoughts.

As therapy progresses, then the topics will start to focus on the underlying difficulties in the client's thinking – that is their dysfunctional thoughts and core beliefs. By this time they will have had some symptomatic relief as a result of the earlier sessions, so they will probably be functioning better in their everyday life, and things that have happened in the intervening weeks should not be so intrusive.

Sometimes you will have become aware of issues that the client needs to address, but which the client is either unaware of, or is avoiding. If this occurs then you will have to bring them up when the agenda is being set.

Homework-setting

The homework topics should usually follow from those that have been discussed in the session. In the early stages, the homework may be very simple – for example, reading through handouts relevant to the sessional topics, or filling in associated questionnaires. Later on in therapy, the homework is often filling in the thought records that are at the heart of cognitive behaviour therapy.

In the middle and later stages of therapy, homework will also consist of doing behavioural experiments. These consist of carefully constructed situations in which the client can collect information to confirm or reject beliefs that they have. They can also be used to test out new beliefs that the client is generating in the course of therapy. New beliefs need externally generated evidence to make them real, rather than just being ideas that may or may not be true.

It can be tempting to spend too much time on dealing with problems during therapy sessions, and not to leave enough time to set homework. It is important that this is resisted. You should be thinking about homework during the session, and about possible homework assignments that could arise out of the discussion.

If the client becomes reluctant to complete the homework assignments, then you must tackle this by raising it as a topic for discussion in one of the sessions. You should then explore what it is that is preventing the client completing the homework assignments. Are they too difficult? Is the client making time to do them, and if not why not? Does the client understand the rationale for doing the assignments, and recognise their importance? Is one of the client's dysfunctional assumptions or core beliefs preventing them from doing the assignments? If so, then it is important that this is tackled as soon as possible.

Reviewing the session and feedback

The final task is to review the session with the client; give any feedback, and ask for feedback from the client. The purpose of this is to ensure that the client has understood what you have said, and that they are able to make sense of what is happening.

To review the session, you ask the client to summarise what has been said. Ask them to do this in a few sentences, just outlining the main points. If there was something in the session that you were not certain that the client understood, then ask the client about it at this stage, to check on their understanding.

It is important for you to give feedback to the client about their progress in the session. If they have worked well then this should be acknowledged by saying something like: 'You worked really well today, perhaps this is a sign that things are getting better.'

If the session was less successful then the difficulties should be acknowledged, but you should also try to find something to praise. For example, 'Today was obviously very difficult for you. You may not have felt that there was much progress, and this may be true. However, you did stick at it, and this is better than you would have managed a few weeks back.' As you can see, the client's difficulties are acknowledged, but they are also given some encouragement. This is important, as it is easy for the client's dysfunctional assumptions to reassert themselves.

You should also ask for feedback about your part in the session. Ask questions such as 'Did you find what I said [did] easy to understand?' or 'Did I do anything that upset or surprised you?' This will help you to get a better understanding of the way you are being perceived by the client, and allow you to make any adjustments necessary to ensure that you are as effective as you can be.

Using cognitive behaviour therapy with groups

Cognitive behaviour therapy can easily be adapted for use in groups. However, it will clearly be more complex and difficult to do. Therefore, you need to have greater skills before attempting to do this. The first thing to decide upon is whether the group is going to be a psycho-educational one, or one that allows more individual discussion of people's problems. This will have implications on the size of the group. A psycho-educational format would allow more people to be dealt with at any one time, but would not give the opportunity for people to discuss their individual problems in the group, and would be more structured. The number of sessions could be decided at the beginning.

However, you could decide to run a group that allows for discussion of individuals' problems. This group would probably take much longer, and it would be harder to predict the exact number of sessions needed at the outset. The therapist should be experienced at running groups and be able to deal with the dynamics of the group as it progresses. While it would be possible to have some variation in the levels of depression, these should not be too great as this would impede the rate at which the group could progress. The use of Socratic dialogue would have to be adapted to include the whole of the group in the questioning process. The setting of homework would probably have to be more generalised as there would not be time to set individual homework, or to review it each week. The time reviewing homework could be varied according to need. The therapist would have to balance the needs of the individual against those of the group. In general, the structure as set out in this manual would have to be followed more closely.

In both models of group work, the sessions would probably need to be one-and-a-half hours long. As with most group work, it would be helpful to have a co-therapist, although this would not be as important in the psycho-educational format, where numbers in the group are less critical, and from as few as three up to 20 people could easily be dealt with. In the group format, allowing more discussion of individuals' problems, the group would operate best if there were between six and eight people. This would provide enough people to allow group discussions to take place, but would be small enough to allow each individual the time to explore their own problems.

Using cognitive behaviour therapy with in-patients

The format described in this manual can easily be adapted to use with in-patients. In general, in-patients are likely to be more depressed, so that at first their progress may be slower.

Initially, they may also find it more difficult to concentrate. This means that you will have to adapt the steps described in the beginning, and you may have to take more sessions at each step, although as therapy progresses the pace will pick up as the client's mood improves. At first, if the client is severely depressed, the sessions may have to be shorter – perhaps only 20 minutes. This is because the client's ability to concentrate will be diminished. It may be necessary for the sessions to be more frequent – up to three times a week – to ensure that any therapeutic gains are not lost between the shortened sessions. You will have to accept that the client will find everything much harder to do. In order to help with this, it will be necessary to try to get the ward staff to cooperate with you. Cooperation is always a two-way thing, so you will have to try to help the ward staff to do the things that they are doing to help the client. Ideally, you and the ward staff should generate the care plan together, so that the different elements fit together to form a coherent whole. The ward staff can often help with the 'homework assignments', so discussing this with both the client and the ward team is essential. The client may need the encouragement or help of the ward staff to complete even the easiest of assignments at the beginning. The net outcome of this is that you may still be able to move at a similar rate to that taken with the less severely depressed out-patient, due to the increased input. If it is not possible to increase the frequency of the sessions, you may have to accept a much slower rate of change, although this may be ameliorated to some extent if the ward staff are able to help in a significant way.

As the client improves, the sessions can become longer and their expectations can increase. Therefore, by the time the client is ready for discharge, you will hopefully be at the same sort of session length and frequency as you would be if all the therapy had been done as out-patient sessions.

Reasons for Failure in Cognitive Behaviour Therapy

Introduction

This section will discuss the possible reasons why cognitive therapy may not seem to be effective in an individual. These can be divided into therapist, patient, structural and external factors. Each of these will be discussed in turn. When considering the reasons for failure of therapy in a particular client, then each of these broad categories should be examined. Remember there may be more than one reason for the failure of the therapy. Some of the reasons that it is not progressing as expected can be resolved, and therefore the therapist needs to be aware of these before commencing therapy. Sometimes possible reasons for failure can be anticipated by the therapist from information gained in the initial assessment – for example, previous therapeutic failure.

Therapist factors

To ensure success the therapist:
- Needs to have an understanding of the cognitive behaviour therapy model, and to believe in it. The therapist needs to be able to convince the client of the effectiveness of the model if they are to be effective.
- Needs to have an empathic approach to the client. Failure in this will lead to the client losing faith in the therapist.
- Must be neither too active nor too inactive, or the therapy will lose its characteristic structure. The therapist must take responsibility for the structure of the therapy.
  If the therapist is too active it prevents the client from developing their own ideas.
  As previously mentioned, this is important as it helps the client to build up their own skills in challenging their dysfunctional thinking processes.

As in most therapies, you should adhere to the therapeutic model as closely as possible to maintain its effectiveness.

Client factors

The client needs to understand and accept the therapeutic model if they are to cooperate appropriately.

If the client is very severely depressed, they may find it difficult to take an active part in therapy. Then the therapist will need to consider whether the patient should be treated in another way, such as with drugs, until they have improved sufficiently. Alternatively, in-patient care with shorter and more frequent sessions could be considered.

The client may not be active enough in therapy. This leads to a dependence on the therapist, and so the collaboration that is essential to success is lost. The therapist need to tackle this.

If the client rejects the cognitive model, the reasons for this should be discussed as sometimes they can be overcome. One of the common reasons for rejecting the cognitive model is that it seems too superficial to some people. This is often because at the beginning the emphasis is on the here and now, and does not seem to address the underlying psychological problems. Explaining that as therapy progresses the emphasis changes to deal with more enduring patterns of thinking and behaving may help the client to accept the model. If, after trying to deal with the client's objections to the cognitive behaviour therapy model, they still do not accept it, then it is best to tell the client that the therapy is not for them, and if possible refer them to an alternative therapist.

If, for some reason, the client does not feel comfortable with you, then they will not be able to enter into the therapeutic relationship. There may be many reasons for this. For example, there may be a characteristic of yours that reminds the client of someone from the past with whom they have had a very negative experience. Whatever the reason, it is usually best to refer the client to another therapist who may be able to conduct cognitive behaviour therapy with them.

Structural factors

Cognitive behaviour therapy is most effective when the structural model is followed. The therapy will suffer if:
- Homework is not set or completed or reviewed. Homework assignments are essential to cognitive behaviour therapy.
- The environment is not appropriate to conducting therapy – for example, if the room is too hot or too cold; there are frequent interruptions; the room isn't sound-proof, or the client does not feel that confidentiality can be guaranteed.
- Sessions are frequently cancelled or rescheduled, by either the therapist or the client. The therapist needs to try to ensure that this does not happen.

External factors

There will be adverse effects if:

- The client has lots of other things going on in their life. If this is the case, then the client cannot concentrate on the therapy and often does not complete homework assignments appropriately. The therapist should discuss this with the client to see if they can reduce their other commitments. If the client is unable to do this, then the therapist should explain that it is probably not the best time to be receiving therapy, and suggest that the therapy be put on hold to a later date when life is less busy for the client.

- Other people in the client's life are resentful of changes that the client is making and put pressure on them to remain as they are or to withdraw from therapy. Dysfunctional assumptions can sometimes be seen as desirable characteristics by other people. For example, assumptions concerning being perfect may be seen as desirable by employers, and changes in the client's attitude to work may not be appreciated. Similarly, the relationship with the client's spouse may be dependent on the client's dysfunctional assumptions. For example, the client may believe that they will only be loved if they always do everything their spouse wants, and changing this may upset the marital relationship. When this is the case, this needs to be discussed, and session(s) with the client and their spouse may be necessary.

- External factors in the therapist's life may interfere with the therapy. The therapist may be able to overcome these by having adequate supervision. If this is not the case, and the client's issues are too close to home, the therapist should explain to the client that they are unable to continue to offer them therapy; explain that it is to do with themselves rather than the client, and arrange for them to be seen by another therapist.

Combining Cognitive Behaviour Therapy with Other Approaches

Introduction

In most cases, cognitive behaviour therapy is effective on its own, and so it should not be necessary to combine it with other approaches. It can, however, be satisfactorily combined with some other therapies, but not others, as detailed below.

Pharmacotherapy

Using cognitive behavioural therapy with drug treatment is usually done when the client is severely depressed, or when drug treatment has not been fully successful in less depressed patients. Controlled trials have demonstrated that the combination of cognitive behaviour therapy and anti-depressants is more effective than either used alone (Jarrett *et al* 1999; Fava *et al* 1988; Bowers 1990; Blackburn *et al* 1981). The use of benzodiazepines, such as diazepam, may interfere with the successful completion of cognitive behaviour therapy. This is because a phenomenon of state-dependant learning applies to the benzodiazepines. In this, the learning that takes place in the drugged state is not transferred adequately to the non-drugged state. Therefore, the use of benzodiazepines should be kept to a minimum.

Other behavioural treatments

These can include such things as social skills training, assertiveness training, or anxiety management training. As they operate on a similar model, they usually combine well with cognitive behaviour therapy. The only consideration is the amount of therapy the client is receiving – too much can lead to overload.

Relaxation and meditational therapies

These usually combine well, and can help with symptom relief as well as giving the client a sense of control of their life. Many meditational therapies arose out of Buddhist philosophy. It is claimed that Buddhism contains many elements that are common to cognitive behaviour therapy, and therefore they fit together well.

Family therapy

Many family therapies can be combined successfully with cognitive behaviour therapy, especially if like behavioural family therapy and systemic family therapy they have affinities with cognitive behaviour therapy. More psychodynamically orientated therapies may not combine as well.

Analytically orientated and client-centred therapies

These do not generally combine well with cognitive behaviour therapy, as the therapeutic relationship is very different and this can lead to difficulties for the client trying to switch between different modes. Cognitive analytical therapy combines some of the elements of cognitive behaviour therapy with an analytical approach. However, again due to the nature of the therapeutic relationship, this may not combine effectively with cognitive behavioural therapy. Therefore, it is best if these approaches are not combined with cognitive behaviour therapy.

Other Models of Depression

Introduction

Cognitive behaviour therapy is based on the cognitive model of depression. There are other models of depression, and these are described briefly below. The various psychological models have often been associated with a particular therapeutic approach, and this is also outlined briefly.

Biological models

Biological models of depression are more implicated in severe and recurrent depressions. Biological factors can be considered to be either innate – that is, genetic – or acquired. Acquired biological factors could include brain damage, as a result of infections, or reactions to drugs, or as part of medical illnesses.

Genetic factors

Studies have shown that the incidence of depression in the general population is between 5 and 30 per cent (Brown *et al* 1977; Wing *et al* 1978). For severe depression, the incidence falls to about 3 to 7 per cent for women and about 1 per cent for men. However, if you have a first degree relative (mother, father, brother, sister, son, or daughter), then the risk is increased to 1 in 10. Twin studies have shown that if one of an identical twin pair has depression, then the other twin has a 40 per cent chance of developing depression. Genetic factors are more relevant in bipolar affective disorder than in unipolar affective disorder. More detailed information concerning the genetics of depressive disorders can be found in *A Handbook of Affective Disorders* (Paykel 1982) or 'Genetics of Depression and Manic Depressive disorders' (McGuffin & Katz, *British Journal of Psychiatry* 155, 1989).

Monoamine hypothesis

Studies have shown that depression is associated with altered functioning of brain neuro-transmitters called monoamines (Shildkraut 1969; Coppen 1967). Levels of noradrenaline and serotonin – the two commonest monoamines – are reduced in the depressed client. Anti-depressants appear to act by increasing the response to these neurotransmitters in the brain. Some drugs used for other medical conditions are known to reduce the levels of monamines in the brain, and these are associated with an increased risk of depression.

Social models

Various social factors are associated with depression:

Gender

Women are twice as likely as men to be diagnosed and treated for depression. The following have been put forward to explain this observation:

1 Women are more likely to seek treatment; are more willing to accept they have emotional symptoms, and are more willing to disclose and discuss them.

2 Men may be less willing to discuss their feelings, and try to suppress their symptoms through the use of drugs and alcohol. Therefore, their use of these substances may be perceived as dependency rather than depression.

3 Women in today's society have the stress of conflicting roles, as they have responsibilities at work and at home.

4 Women may be more prone to hormonal influences. They can develop illnesses following changes in their hormonal levels.

Adversity in early life

Research by Brown and Moran (1994) has shown that various events in early life predisposed people to depression. These events included:

1 Physical sexual contact, excluding willing contact with unrelated peers, in teenage years.

2 Parental indifference: physical or emotional neglect; parental lack of interest or involvement in material care, schoolwork, friends and so on.

3 Physical abuse: violence shown towards the subject by a household member, such as actual beatings, threats with knives and so on.

4 Loss of a parent. Death or separation followed by inadequate parental care.

Current stressful life events

Brown and Harris (1978) and Brown *et al* (1988, 1995) have shown that depressive episodes are often preceded by stressful life events. These can include:

1 Severe, acute life events: acute life situations of recent onset that carry or potentially carry a serious long-term threat to the emotional wellbeing of the individual. Losses can be interpersonal, material, or loss of a cherished idea (for example, finding out about a child's delinquency)

2 Chronic life difficulty: a life situation lasting at least four weeks that carries or potentially carries a long-term threat to the individual's emotional wellbeing.

3 Poor quality social support: this is particularly important at a time of crisis, or in the context of life events or a life difficulty. It may itself be a provoking life event or life difficulty; sometimes the anticipated buffering against a life event is not experienced.

Maintaining factors for depressive illness

Research by Brown and Moran, (1994), Ronalds *et al* (1997), and Harris *et al* (1999) has shown that various factors maintain a state of depression. These include:

1 Further negative life events
2 Persistent poor quality social support
3 Poor coping style:
  - Self blame and helplessness
  - Denial of problems
  - Inability to solve problems
  - Blaming others or external events.
4 Inability to obtain adequate social support:
  - Fear of intimacy
  - Denial of the need for intimacy
  - Enmeshed intimate relationship.
5 Low educational level.

These social factors can be put together to give a social model of depression in non-psychotic depressive disorder, as in Figure 3.

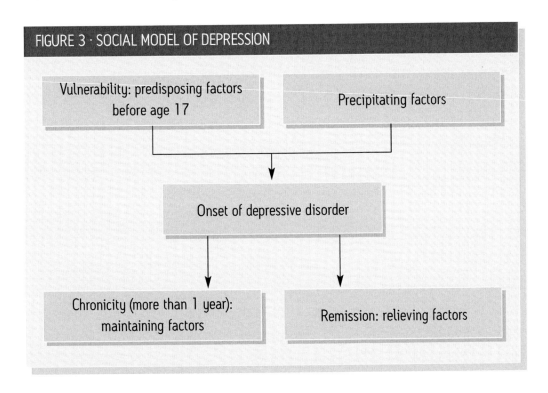

FIGURE 3 · SOCIAL MODEL OF DEPRESSION

Vulnerability: predisposing factors before age 17

Precipitating factors

Onset of depressive disorder

Chronicity (more than 1 year): maintaining factors

Remission: relieving factors

Psychological models

A wide range of psychological models have been developed to explain depression.

Psychodynamic

Freud (1917) viewed depression as the long-term outcome of childhood problems. If, as a child, an individual's needs were not met, or they suffered an ego-damaging experience, they might become dependent on others for the maintenance of their self-esteem. Other analysts have extended these psychodynamic theories. For example, the psychodynamic model has been extended to include the quality of relationships with significant others in early childhood. This became the 'object relations theory', and Bowlby's work on early attachment has been integrated into this (Bowlby 1983).

The psychodynamic model of therapy encourages the client to talk about whatever comes into their head, which will encourage repressed thoughts and unconscious preoccupations to emerge, possibly in a distorted or symbolic way. These can then be brought back to consciousness and the client can work with them. This process is known as free association. The client is allowed to set their own agenda; define their problems, and set their own objectives. The therapist needs to be able to tolerate silences and renounce the active role of the 'doer'.

The therapist will feel the need to say something, but the silences can be used to develop empathy and non-verbal communication skills, and to encourage clarifying and rephrasing. This has the curious effect of strengthening the relationship and allowing the client time to talk. The question now becomes 'What do I need to say?', instead of 'What did they want to hear?'. The therapeutic outcome depends greatly on the therapist being able to tolerate painful silences and disclosures. The therapist should not attempt to sort out the client's confusion, but allow the client the space to express themselves. The client's behaviour, including their interpersonal style and symptoms, expresses the client's inner world; their sense of themselves and their perception of others. The person's inner world is shaped by their past experiences, and this gives meaning to their current experience. The psychodynamic approach is only interested in the past if it has great effect on the present.

Person-centred therapy

Carl Rogers, the developer of person-centred therapy, believed the development of the person's creative potential and capacity for self-understanding promoted the ability to cope with life in a constructive manner (Rogers 1977). When a person is able to find their inner strength they can begin to believe in their ability to make responsible decisions that shape their life. The therapist, in effect, hands control and decision-making to the client. The aim of person-centred therapy is to enable the client to become fully functioning and to reach their full potential. For this to occur, the therapist must create an environment where growth is promoted. Clients will then be motivated by positive, not negative, forces and therefore will not need to rely on maladaptive coping skills. Rogers' philosophy implies that in order for this to be an effective relationship, the therapist must be a fully functioning person. The following key concepts ensure that the therapy has the optimum chance of success.

Genuineness

The therapist must allow the client to witness their genuine feelings; therefore they have to listen to what the client is telling them. The client needs to view the therapist as a person who has a real interest in what the client is discussing. This involves congruence between what the therapist is saying and their non-verbal communication. Appropriate and frequent eye contact, and an encouraging tone of voice reassures the client and initiates an atmosphere of openness and honesty.

Acceptance

The therapist needs to provide a non-judgmental arena for the client to talk about their behaviour. The acceptance of this behaviour, and unconditional positive regard are essential in acknowledging the client as they are, and valuing them as such. The therapist is concerned for the client, despite maladaptive coping mechanisms or destructive behaviour. The positive feelings of the therapist are not influenced by the client's behaviour.

Empathy

Empathy is the sensing of the client's feelings, which allows the therapist to step into the client's world and understand their feelings. The therapist can then clarify what the client is experiencing, and by communicating this back help the client to view their feelings more objectively. Empathy allows the therapist to experience similar emotions to those of the client, and helps to strengthen the relationship between them.

Person-centred therapy encourages the client to become an active participant in their own therapy by advocating self-responsibility and self-determinism; it encourages them to progress towards self-actualisation. Rogers believed that when growth and fulfilment are optimised, a person is fully functional. They become able to participate in life, actively seek new experiences, and take responsibility for the decisions they make.

Therapeutic steps

Part 2

Introduction

Set agenda – *5 minutes*

This week's task: Describe the model of depression and therapy – *40 minutes*

Review session – *5 to 10 minutes*

Set homework – *5 to 10 minutes*

Materials needed – *Handouts 1 & 2 for Step 1* and also *Handout 1 for Step 2*

Introduction

In this first session, the main aim is to describe the cognitive behaviour therapy model of depression and the format of the therapy. All of the information that you need to do this is contained in Part 1. You will have seen that the sessions have a definite structure, which should be used in this first session. Therefore, you should start by setting the agenda. This will include the usual things, with the exception of reviewing homework as, this being the first session, none will have been set. Therefore, this week's agenda will cover this week's task (describing the cognitive behaviour therapy model and therapy structure); reviewing the session, and setting homework.

Set agenda

As this is the first time that you and the client will have attempted to set an agenda, you will need to explain the reasons for agenda-setting. Establishing the collaborative nature of the treatment is important, and agenda-setting is part of this. Also, at this point you cannot know what has happened since the client was last seen, so cannot judge what is most important to the client at this stage. Agenda-setting also enables the therapy to develop a focus, and be more targeted at the client's symptoms and at the skills that they need to acquire to overcome their difficulties. As therapy progresses, the setting of the agenda becomes easier, but in the early sessions you will have to take an active role. This is because the client may not be aware of the style of therapy, and because, at the beginning, you will have lots of new information and skills to impart that you will wish to have on the agenda. Also, this will provide an opportunity for you to model some of the skills needed to work collaboratively, for the client. This is done by behaving in a way that promotes collaboration such as Socratic dialogue and asking for and giving feedback.

At this stage you will not usually have any difficulties in agreeing the agenda. However, this may not always be the case. If you and the client cannot agree, it is often best to go with the client's agenda. If it turns out that it is not possible to achieve what was agreed then it is possible to renegotiate the agenda with the client. This allows the client to learn from their mistakes, which can be a very powerful experience.

The agenda in cognitive therapy tends to have a set format, within which the client decides what to include, in discussion with the therapist. The agenda will always include a review of homework; specific tasks for the day; reviewing the session, and setting homework for the next week. This format needs to be explained to the client, and then within this you need to negotiate the specific tasks for today's session. It is suggested that these should focus on discussing the cognitive behaviour therapy model of depression and explaining the therapeutic style.

This week's task

Describing the cognitive behaviour therapy model and style of therapy forms the core of this week's task. First, use the information in Part 1 to describe the cognitive model of depression. This will cover the interactive nature of negative automatic thoughts, mood and behaviour, and their mutual reinforcement. It is usually best to start the description of the cognitive behaviour therapy model at the negative automatic thoughts end, as this is the most accessible to the client. Then work backwards to dysfunctional assumptions, explaining the way these cause the negative automatic thoughts. Describe the nature of dysfunctional assumptions, and core beliefs – it is not necessary to go into detail at this stage. Describe the role of external events in activating dysfunctional assumptions, and of early life events in the establishment of dysfunctional assumptions and core beliefs. Again, detail is not required at this stage.

It is often helpful to draw out the model as in *Handout 1 for Step 1* as you describe it to the client. If you have sufficient information about the client, you could personalise it for them by using some of the negative automatic thoughts and dysfunctional assumptions they have. It is unlikely that you will have this information unless you have seen the client on several previous occasions.

After you have covered the model, describe the nature of the therapy. Again use the information in Part 1 to help with this. You should also use *Handout 2 for Step 1* to help with this.

Review the session

In reviewing the session you are doing several things. You are checking that the information you gave to the client was understood. You will also get an idea how the client interprets the information, which may tell you something about their thinking style, and how it affects their mood. It will also force the client to think through what has been said, which will help it to become more firmly embedded in their thinking. Finally, the review will allow you to correct anything that was misunderstood and make changes to the way you present information, if it becomes clear that the way you have been doing things is not easily accessible to the client.

How you review the session also helps to establish collaboration between you and the client, as you ask them to tell you what they think was covered in the session. If the client gets it basically right, then all is well. If they do not seem to have understood the information, then you have to be tactful in how you handle this, as the client will undoubtedly interpret any criticism negatively, which could further activate their negative automatic thoughts and dysfunctional assumptions. You should try to pick out the things they said that reflect what you think went on, and then also mention the other important things you covered. For example, if the client does not seem to have remembered anything about the role of dysfunctional assumptions and activating events, then you should say something like: 'That's right, we did talk about the role of negative automatic thoughts, but we also talked about the role of dysfunctional assumptions, do you remember?'

You should also remember to ask for feedback on your presentation to the client. The client is likely to be a little hesitant to criticise you, so if you noticed something during the session to which the client reacted untowardly, then you could mention this. Ask them if there was anything that upset them about the session. If the general style of the therapy causes them concern – perhaps they had been expecting something very different – then suggest that they read through the handout so that they can reflect on it and then discuss it at the next session.

Set homework

It is important that the client understands that homework is essential to the effectiveness of cognitive behaviour therapy, and it is your responsibility to explain why the homework has been set.

The setting of the homework should usually be done in a collaborative way. The subject matter will generally arise from the discussion in the session. Therefore, in this first session the homework will usually centre on further identification of the pattern of the client's depressive illness.

If there are difficulties when setting homework, then these should be discussed with the client. They may feel that the homework you have set is too much, or too little, or that it is too difficult. If they have particular problems, these should be explored, and if they appear to be reasonable then changes should be made to the homework task.

However, if following the discussion it seems that the homework assignment is reasonable, then every encouragement should be given to the client to continue with it. You should explain that homework is not a test, and that they will not be criticised if they are unable to complete it.

Remember clients often underestimate their capabilities as a result of their depressive symptoms.

This week, the homework will be quite simple. The client should be asked to read through *Handouts 1 and 2 for Step 1* and also *Handout 1 for Step 2,* in preparation for the next session.

The Cognitive Model of Depression

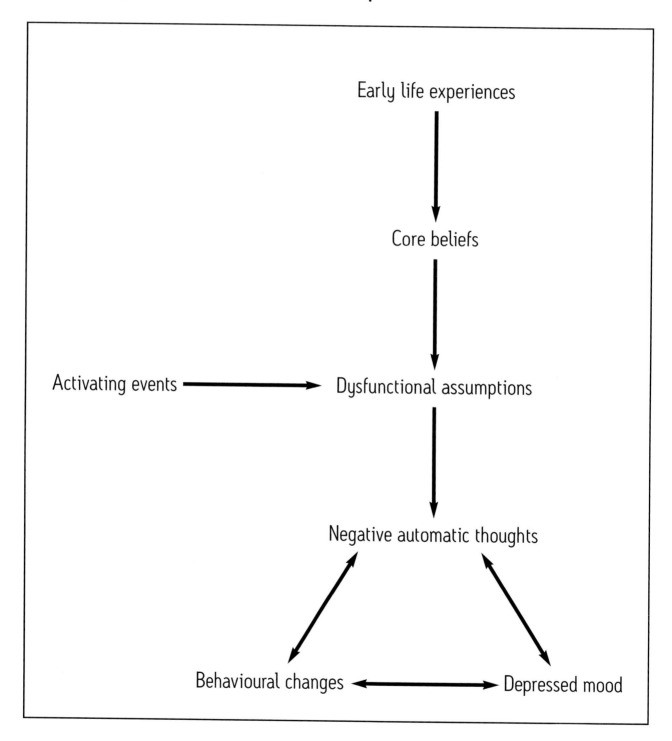

Introduction to Cognitive Behaviour Therapy

The treatment that you will receive in the coming weeks is based on cognitive behaviour therapy. Cognitive behaviour therapy has developed over the last 30 years, and has been proven to be an effective treatment for many psychological disorders. There have been many research studies that have demonstrated its effectiveness in depressive illness.

In this style of treatment you and the therapist work together to overcome your depression. Understanding the thoughts you have is seen as central to understanding your depression. In cognitive behaviour therapy, disturbance in mood is seen as being caused by distortions in your thinking patterns.

Typically, cognitive behaviour therapy takes between 12 and 25 sessions. The sessions are usually one hour long. The therapy focuses on current problems that you have. In order to make the most effective use of the therapy sessions, it is usual to structure them. A session typically consists of the following:

1 Setting the agenda
2 Reviewing the previous week's homework
3 Working on one or two problems
4 Setting homework
5 Review of the session.

Setting the agenda involves deciding what to focus on during the session. This style of therapy encourages collaboration, so you and the therapist will decide jointly what will be covered in each session.

Between each session you will be set 'homework'. This is because it is important to maximise the effect of the therapy by carrying on the work between the sessions. Just as you discuss what to focus on in the sessions, you will also decide jointly with the therapist the nature of the homework.

At the end of the session, you and the therapist will spend some time reviewing what has gone on, and any thoughts you may have had concerning this. This enables you and the therapist to check through what has been covered in the session, and ensure that you have understood things.

You may have already noticed that when you are depressed you have more negative thoughts, and that your levels of energy and motivation are both low. This in turn leads to decreased activity. You will learn how to increase your activity and to recognise, and eventually challenge and overcome, your negative thoughts. This will then lead to an improvement in your depressed mood.

In order for you to be able to do this, the therapy consists of 10 steps. You will work through the steps with your therapist at a pace that you and the therapist decide upon. Throughout this treatment process you will be given handouts, like this one, to help you understand how to overcome your depression.

Step 2 · Identifying the Client's Depression

Introduction

Set agenda – *5 minutes*

Review homework – *5 to 10 minutes*

This week's task: Define the client's depression – *35 minutes*

Review session – *5 to 10 minutes*

Set homework – *5 to 10 minutes*

Materials needed – *Handouts 2 & 3 for Step 2*

Introduction

The purpose of this step is to help the client to:

1 Identify symptoms of depression and understand how they affect their life
2 Generate their own personal profile of depression
3 Establish boundaries to their depression, which will enable them to establish ownership and eventually control of their symptoms.

Set agenda

This will be only the second agenda that you and the client set together. This means that you will have to take an active part in the agenda-setting. You may have to explain the structure of the session again, but this is best left to when you review the homework, as it will be covered then anyway. The agenda will follow the same format as before, but this time the first item will be to review the homework. The main task this week will be to define the client's depression. After the agenda has been set, move straight on to this.

Review homework from last week

Ask the client how they got on with their homework. Check whether they have any queries about the handouts, especially *Handout 2 for Step 1* of the cognitive behavioural model of therapy. Deal with these as necessary. If they have questions about *Handout 1 for Step 2*, then this can be dealt with in the main task of the day.

This week's task

1 Identifying symptoms of depression and understanding how the symptoms affect their life

Describe the symptoms of depression using *Handouts 1 and 2 for Step 2* as an aid. Stop, at times, to allow the client to take in what you have said, and ask them if any of the things you have said apply to them.

You should also use any other knowledge of depression and associated symptoms that you may have, especially if you are aware of the client's symptoms and can help them to identify them.

2 Generating their own personal profile of depression

After describing various symptoms of depression, and having identified some of the patient's symptoms, ask them to start to use *Handout 3 for Step 2* and to begin to fill this in. You will see that the questionnaire is divided into various sections. It is usually helpful to stop at the end of each section and discuss its contents with the client. Help them to associate and/or identify with the symptoms in the section, and explore whether they trigger off other ideas about their own symptoms. Try to concentrate on one section at a time, and get the client to rate the importance and severity of particular symptoms. Some may not be that severe, but may well be important to the client.

The importance of particular symptoms could be rated on a 0 to 5 scale, with zero being the least important and five the most important. If the client feels happier with a different scale, then get them to design their own.

The severity scale is usually best done on a 0 to 100 scale, as this can be talked about as percentages that are usually easily understood by clients.

While the client is completing the questionnaire it will become apparent that they do not experience all of the symptoms, or that some of the symptoms are not particularly severe. You can use this information to help the client recognise that in some areas they are still functioning reasonably normally. These positive aspects should be pointed out to enable the client to recognise that things are not all bad.

By doing this, the client will be able to place some boundaries on their depression, and this can then start to act as a focus for overcoming their symptoms. They can be advised to try to maximise their use of the areas of their life that are still functioning well, as a way of improving their mood and increasing self-esteem.

You are unlikely to finish the questionnaire in the session; in fact, you may not have proceeded that far. This is not important, as completion of the questionnaire is a good task to set as homework.

What do I do if the client is unable to participate?

If the client is unable to participate, it may be helpful to feedback some of the symptoms you know that they have, and ask them to talk about these. Use *Handout 3 for Step 2* to see how the symptoms that you are aware of relate to this.

If the client is still unable to become involved, it is necessary to explore the reasons with them. Ask them questions like 'What is stopping you?'; 'Is there something bothering you?'; or 'Is there something wrong with the approach, or with the way I am doing things?'

If they are unable to explain what is wrong, consider if they are too depressed at this stage to benefit from this approach, and consider referral.

Review the session

Check that the client has understood what you have covered in the session, and that they know how to carry on with identifying their profile of depression. Ask them how they feel about the therapy, especially the style of therapy. Check with them that they feel comfortable with the way that you are dealing with things. If there are problems and they can be dealt with quickly, do so; if not make a mental note and try to deal with the problem in a future session. If it is a major problem, then it will have to be put on the agenda for the next session to prevent it interfering with the progress of the therapy.

Set homework

As mentioned above, it is unlikely that you will have completed filling in *Handout 3 for Step 2*, so it will make a good subject for the homework. If you did manage to complete it, then get the client to review it; think about what they wrote, and make any necessary changes.

What is Depression?

Depression is an illness that:

- People cannot see. However, it is an illness as cancer is an illness.
- Affects the mind but has effects on your body.
- Will affect one in five people during their lifetime.
- In 80 per cent of cases can be treated successfully. The remaining 20 per cent can receive some relief of their symptoms.
- Can affect anyone from any background. However, women are twice as prone to depression as men.

Depression is not:

- Your fault.
- Something 'you should pull yourself together about'.
- The same as having an 'off day' or feeling a bit unhappy.
- Affecting you because you are weak and you cannot sort it out.
- The step on to other forms of serious mental illness.

Depression takes many forms. We have all experienced some of the symptoms of depression, as we have all felt sad. However, depression is likely to be diagnosed when the symptoms become more severe and widespread. Although the change may come gradually, the depressed person is different from the way they were before the onset of their illness – perhaps even the opposite of their usual self. There are many examples of this change: the successful businessman who believes he is on the brink of bankruptcy; the devoted mother who cannot cope with her children; the gourmet who cannot stand food, or the extrovert who becomes withdrawn.

The depressed person avoids rather than seeks pleasure. Instead of caring for themselves, they neglect themselves and their appearance. Their instinct to survive may give way to a desire to end their life. Passivity and withdrawal replace the drive to succeed.

The most obvious and typical sign of depression is a depressed mood: gloomy, low, sad and apathetic. You may have trouble with sleep – in getting off to sleep; waking during the night or early in the morning, or being unable to return to sleep. Or, feeling constantly tired, you may sleep more than usual. You may find yourself crying even when there seems to be nothing to cry about, or you may find it impossible to cry when a truly sad event occurs. You may lose your appetite and lose weight, or eat more than you do normally and gain weight.

Typically, when you are depressed you tend to see yourself in a very negative way. You become pessimistic about yourself, about the world and about your future. You may believe that you are helpless

What is Depression?

and alone in the world, and blame yourself for trivial faults or shortcomings. Often, you may have trouble making decisions or getting yourself to carry out decisions you have made. You may lose interest in what is going on around you, and not get satisfaction out of activities you used to enjoy.

Sometimes you may be depressed without showing the usual sad, moody, dejected feeling. You may complain instead of physical symptoms, or suffer from alcoholism or drug addiction. When a person always seems tired or bored with what they are doing, they may actually be depressed. When bright children do poorly in school over a period of time, this too may point to depression. An overly active child may be compensating for an underlying depression.

When you are depressed, you may feel that you have lost something important to you even when this is not actually the case. Being depressed, you may believe you are a 'loser' and will always be a loser, that you are worthless and bad, and perhaps not fit to live.

Thoughts of suicide can be common when you are depressed. This is especially the case when you start feeling worthless and cannot see a future for yourself. If your depression becomes more severe, and your view of yourself and your future becomes more hopeless, you may start to feel suicidal. If this occurs it is important to talk to your therapist or doctor about it as soon as possible.

Causes of Depression

The treatment that you will undertake with your therapist can help you overcome your depression. However, it is important to be able to use this understanding to manage events in your life that influence your depression. Understanding your depression and where it comes from is the first step. This handout will identify causes and enable you to relate these to your own life.

Causes of depression are usually divided into three groups: biological, sociological and psychological. The causes of your depression may belong to one or all of these groups.

Biological

- Studies have shown that depression can run in families, in particular between close relatives. These genetic factors cannot be changed; however, you can learn how to deal with difficult thoughts and feelings and so reduce their impact.
- There are physical factors that influence depression. These can be greatly assisted by the prescribing of anti-depressant medication, and you will benefit from taking this medication if it has been prescribed for you.

Sociological

- Gender: Women are twice as likely as men to be diagnosed and treated for depression. This is influenced by women often being more willing to discuss thoughts and feelings; men generally tend to suppress their feelings, possibly with alcohol or drugs. Women are also more prone to hormonal influences.
- Life history: Growing up in an environment where depression is present can influence the way you perceive problems. You witness the ways that your family use when dealing with difficulties. This treatment will show you methods to challenge these and to learn more effective techniques. Events in early childhood have a great impact on our lives as adults. Lack of social support; abusive relationships; physical or emotional neglect, and tragic life events can influence your mood and your perception of yourself and others.

Psychological

- There are various psychological theories of depression. Some emphasise the role of experiences in early life as being important in depression in later life, due to the establishment of various maladaptive patterns of thinking or of responding to events. The cognitive theory of depression is illustrated in *Handout 1 for Step 1*.
This theory suggests that people develop maladaptive patterns of thinking as a result of earlier experiences, especially in childhood. These faulty patterns cause distortions in thinking that can then lead to depression.

Symptoms of Depression

Emotional

	Tick if present	Rank in order of importance	Severity 0–100 per cent
Things do not seem right.			
You cannot find anything about your life that brings you hope or joy.			
Trying to smile is such an effort and does not come naturally.			
You are often worrying or feeling anxious.			
Everything feels like it just won't work, even if you try.			
You have a sense that something awful is going to happen, but you do not quite know what.			
Everything seems dull and grey. Even sunny days seem dull.			
You are on edge most of the time.			
When you look around, people seem happy and getting on with their lives, unlike you.			

Physical

You feel as if you cannot breathe — it's as if you are suffocating.			
Your feelings appear blunted. Food has no interest for you, even the foods you previously enjoyed. Music does not touch you. You do not care how your clothes look.			
You have no wish to put on make-up/have a shave.			
You seem to have lots of physical symptoms. For example, you have headaches or stomach pains, and your GP cannot find anything wrong. You start to think something is seriously wrong with you.			
Your sleep is disturbed. You may find it harder to get off to sleep, or may wake up early. You feel tired by day, and may want to sleep to escape the way you feel.			
It is an effort to prepare or eat food, and it is something that holds no enjoyment for you.			

Symptoms of Depression

	Tick if present	Rank in order of importance	Severity 0–100 per cent

Interpersonal

	Tick if present	Rank in order of importance	Severity 0–100 per cent
Talking to anyone is difficult. What you say does not sound interesting or relevant.			
You feel distant from people around you, as if you are just watching, not taking part in life.			
You've been avoiding friends, and made excuses when asked about this.			
You have lost interest in sex and any physical display of affection. It all just seems a waste of time.			
You try to avoid spending time with family and friends, preferring to be on your own.			
You prefer not to leave home, and when you do you hope that you will not meet anyone you know. You think they will see how bad you feel on the inside.			

Behavioural

You find you cry easily at things you would normally cope with.			
You find life painful, and drinking or drugs help to stop it hurting for a while.			
You no longer enjoy the things you used to, and do not try to find things to fill your day.			
You comfort eat to help fill the empty space in your life.			

Cognitive

You feel as if everything is slowing down.			
You find it hard to focus, and put off making decisions.			
Concentrating is hard, you feel yourself drifting off.			
You think about death often, and see it as a way out of how you feel.			
You have difficulty remembering what day it is, and seem to forget things easily.			

Symptoms of Depression

	Tick if present	Rank in order of importance	Severity 0–100 per cent

Self-esteem

You feel like everything you do will be wrong.			
You focus on all the things that have gone wrong in your life.			
Your clothes reflect the way you feel: choosing dark, drab clothes.			
You cannot remember the last time you laughed.			
You do not feel able to cope with your job or daily activities like you did before.			
You plan only for today, you cannot think about tomorrow.			

Motivation

Getting out of bed seems like a struggle and not really worth it.			
You find you cannot keep on top of things at home – for example, washing and cleaning.			
You cannot be bothered to make an effort with yourself. For example, you wear clothes that you can 'hide in'.			

Other symptoms (Insert other symptoms not listed above.)

Step 3 · Increasing the Client's Activity

Introduction

Session 1

Set agenda – *5 to 10 minutes*

Review homework – *5 to 10 minutes*

This week's task: Introduce activity scheduling – *5–10 minutes*

Demonstrate use of daily and weekly activity sheets – *10–20 minutes*

Review session – *5 to 10 minutes*

Set homework – *5 to 10 minutes*

Materials needed – One copy of *Handout 1*, or seven copies of *Handout 2*. One copy of *Handout 3*

Session 2

Set agenda – *5 minutes*

Review homework – *5 to 10 minutes*

This week's task: Discuss how to overcome inactivity using Handouts 3, 4, 5 and 6 – *30 minutes*

Review session – *5 to 10 minutes*

Set homework – *5 to 10 minutes*

Materials needed – Further copies of *Handout 1 or 2*, and one copy each of *Handouts 4, 5 and 6 for Step 3*

Introduction

When people become depressed, a vicious circle develops. Depression slows people down, they feel tired and withdrawn. This affects them both physically and mentally. As a result, they do less and find everyday tasks hard work. They start to blame themselves for what they see as failings, calling themselves lazy. They start to feel they are incompetent, and that they will never get back to their normal selves. This in turn leads to further feelings of depression, and so the circle continues. So, in this step you are to help the client to increase their activity levels. You will explain to them why increasing their activity levels will help, and discuss the difficulties they may encounter.

The first task is to teach them how to monitor their activity, and then to plan for future days' activities, using the schedules provided (*Handouts 1 and 2*).

This step will take at least two sessions, and probably longer. The first session should concentrate on the rationale for monitoring, and demonstrate the use of the activity schedule in recording what they are currently doing. The second, and possibly subsequent, session should focus on the client's plans to increase their activity.

Session 1

Set agenda

Discuss with the client what the session is to include. It will begin, as all sessions should, with reviewing the homework from the previous session. Then the tasks for this week should be decided upon. Suggest to the client that concentrating on their levels of activity could be a useful thing to do. Check that they do not have any important issues that they need to discuss. If they do, then you will have to find some space on the agenda for this.

Review homework from last week

Check that the client has been able to complete the homework from the previous session. Deal with any difficulties they encountered there and then, if possible. If the difficulties were significant, it may mean that you will have to renegotiate the agenda to deal with them today. Sometimes, even a major problem does not need to be dealt with straight away, and if this is the case it is best if it is left for another time. You will have to remember this, and introduce the problem when you think it would be suitable.

This week's task

Start this part of the session by explaining the rationale for activity-scheduling. Table 3 describes reasons you can use to justify the need for the client to increase their activity. Discuss each one with the client, and try to get their views on what you say. At this stage their negative automatic thoughts may make it hard for them to see the advantages of increasing their activity, so you may have to spend a little time trying to persuade them of the value of activity.

If necessary, explain to them how their negative automatic thoughts are influencing their perspective. To overcome this, it is sometimes necessary to have them recall how things were when they were not depressed. Another way of helping them overcome their negative automatic thoughts is to depersonalise the thoughts: suggest they think about what advice they might give to someone else. Clients are often more positive about other people. In the end, you may have to suggest that even though they cannot see any advantages to increasing their activity, you would like them to give it a go anyway. What have they to lose?

TABLE 3 · REASONS ACTIVITY IS WORTHWHILE

1 · Activity makes people feel better. Becoming more active is a way to break the vicious circle. It does this by taking the client's mind off how they are feeling. It can give a sense of having some control over their lives that many depressed people have lost. In addition, they may even enjoy what they do.

---

2 · Activity makes people feel less tired. In depression, inactivity actually makes the client feel more tired. So, being more active will actually help to relieve the symptoms of tiredness and lethargy.

---

3 · Activity motivates people to do more. Doing things when they are depressed makes the client want to do more. Again, this helps to break the vicious circle.

---

4 · Activity improves people's ability to think. As clients start to do things, it helps them regain their perspective and think more clearly.

---

5 · It improves relationships. People who matter to the client will probably be pleased to see their depressed friend or relative doing more.

In spite of the advantages described in Table 3, getting going again is not easy. This is because the negative thoughts, which are typical of depression, stand in the way. Thoughts such as 'I won't enjoy it', or 'I'll get it all wrong', or 'I will not be able to do it as it's too hard' fill the person's mind. The net effect of this is to stop them trying to do anything.

To overcome the inactivity, it is first necessary to find out what the person is doing (sometimes this is much more than the client gives themselves credit for). In order to do this, you will need to instruct them in using the activity schedule (*Handouts 1 and 2*). After this, the aim is to build up the client's activity. To do this, it will be necessary to look at the things that stop them undertaking tasks. It will also be necessary to help the client identify the negative thoughts that stop them, and begin to challenge them. Most depressed clients believe that they are doing almost nothing at all. They think that they do not gain any enjoyment from anything they do. This makes it difficult for them to organise themselves.

To help them overcome this, they need to start to use an activity schedule. This is simply an hour-by-hour record of the client's activities. The client is instructed to fill in the schedule with their activities over the coming week. Two different kinds of activity schedule are provided – a daily one and a weekly one. The therapist must choose the most appropriate one to use.

You then need to instruct the client how to fill in the schedule, using the information below. You should demonstrate this using an actual schedule. Try to think of an activity that is relevant to them, or that they currently do. If you are not aware of anything, try asking the client if they have an activity that they might wish to do, and then use this as your example.

There are two stages to filling in the record:

1 Recording the actual activities hour by hour.
2 Giving each activity a rating for pleasure and achievement, usually using a 0 to10 scale, though clients can devise their own scale if they prefer to. Scores of 10 for pleasure or achievement would mean that it had been extremely enjoyable, or given the client a great sense of achievement. Similarly a score of 0 for pleasure or achievement means it was unpleasurable or gave them no sense of achievement.

Important points in filling out the schedule:
● It is important for the client to rate their activities for pleasure and achievement at the time, not in retrospect. When people are depressed, negative and unpleasant events are more easily noticed and remembered. The good things are blotted out by a sort of global pessimism. Immediate ratings will help them to become sensitive to even small degrees of pleasure and achievement, which might otherwise go unnoticed.

- The client should be instructed to rate according to how difficult the particular activity is for them at that particular time, not how difficult it is for them normally. When people are depressed, things that would normally be very easy become difficult, so clients have to give themselves credit when they achieve them. This point needs to be stressed to the client, as they are unlikely to see it this way.
- The activity schedule will give you and the client hard data on what the client is actually doing and enjoying, and so challenge the belief that nothing goes well for them. You and they are quite likely to find that they are more active and competent than they assumed, and that they are enjoying themselves more than they thought. Even if that is not the case, you will have valuable evidence to hand to assist you to help the client find out what is getting in their way.

Figure 4 is an example of an activity schedule covering a few hours.

FIGURE 4 · ACTIVITY SCHEDULE

TIME	ACTIVITY	Achievement 0–10	Pleasure 0–10
8–9	Lay in bed	0	2
9–10	Got up, washed, dressed and had a cup of tea.	4	2
10–11	Friend visited	2	6*
11–12	Did some ironing	7**	2

* Note even when depressed, clients can still get some pleasure.
** This activity is scored highly on achievement, because it took the person a lot of effort to motivate themselves.

As you can see, the level of detail need not be high, so it is easy for the client to fill in. Also, note that simple everyday things are the stuff of activity charts – that is, the things we take for granted, without even considering them actions. Describing the rationale for increasing activity, and demonstrating the use of the activity schedule, will probably take up the whole session.

Review the session

Check with the client what they have learnt during the session, and whether there are any problems with what has been covered. Ask for feedback on how they perceived you. At this stage, it is important that the client feels comfortable with the way you communicate. If appropriate, you can adjust your approach for the next session. Sometimes, comments about how you do things are really comments on the style of cognitive therapy, and an explanation as to why you proceed in this way often suffices.

Set homework

Ask the client to fill in a schedule of their activities over the next week. If they are severely depressed, do not expect too much, and ensure the client is aware that you do not expect a masterpiece. You will need to give them copies of either *Handout 1 or 2 for Step 3*, depending on how much detail you think the client will need. *Handout 2* is probably easier to use, but as it covers only one day you would have to give them seven copies to cover the week. You should also give them *Handout 3 for Step 3* to help them complete the activity schedule.

Session 2
Set agenda

The agenda will follow the same format as before – that is, reviewing the homework; agreeing this week's tasks; reviewing the session, and setting homework. This week's tasks will focus on ways of helping the client to increase their levels of activity.

Review homework from last week

Check how the client got on with their homework; see what difficulties they had, and be sure to address them in the session.

This week's tasks

Now that you know how the client is spending their time, the next step is to plan each day in advance, and to include the sort of activities that give them a sense of enjoyment and achievement. To do this, it will be necessary to look at the things that stop them undertaking tasks. It will also be necessary to help the client to identify the negative thoughts that stop them, and begin to challenge them.

The client should be instructed to spend a few minutes each evening planning for the next day. They should be advised to pick a time when they will not be busy, tired or distracted. They should plan the next day hour by hour. Sometimes, if the person is very depressed, they will find it hard to fill the whole day with activities. If this is the case, they should be asked to estimate how much time they think they could plan, and then encouraged to do a little more, as they tend to underestimate their capabilities. They need to balance their activities between those that are easy and enjoyable, and those that are more challenging, but not too difficult. Easy and enjoyable activities could include sitting having a cup of tea or watching the television. More challenging ones might include small household tasks, such as washing the pots or cleaning the car. They should keep the plan simple at the beginning, and slowly build up to more difficult and challenging things. There is no rush – remember, Rome wasn't built in a day!

The client may be reluctant to keep an activity schedule. Table 4 contains three reasons why it is a good idea. These points should be communicated to the client. Remember, everything you ask the client to do should have a reason behind it, and you should feel comfortable communicating these to them.

TABLE 4 · THREE REASONS FOR KEEPING TO A PLAN OF ACTIVITY

1 · Structuring their time will allow them to feel that they are taking control of their life again, and give them a sense of purpose.

---

2 · The framework will prevent them from sinking in a swamp of minor decisions, and help them to keep going even when they are feeling down.

---

3 · Once the day's activities are laid out in writing, they will seem less overwhelming. The client will have broken down the day into a series of manageable units, rather than being faced with a long, shapeless stretch of time that they must somehow fill.

Spend some of the session helping the client to fill in the activity schedule for the next day or two. Ensure that they adhere to the points you covered in the previous week.

Run through *Handouts 4, 5 and 6*, and discuss methods the client can use to help them increase their activity.

Review the session

Check with the client what they have learnt during the session, and whether they have any problems with what has been covered. Ask for feedback on how they perceived your involvement.

Set homework

Ask the client to continue to use the activity schedules till the next session. Give them enough copies to do this. Ask the client to read through the handouts. Ensure that they know that the activity schedule is a way of planning their activity, and also a way of recording the sense of pleasure and achievement that their activity gives them.

Weekly Activity Schedule

	MONDAY	TUESDAY	WEDNESDAY	THURSDAY	FRIDAY	SATURDAY	SUNDAY
8–9							
9–10							
10–11							
11–12							
12–1							
1–2							
2–3							
3–4							
4–5							
5–6							
6–7							
7–8							
8–9							
9–10							

NOTE: Grade activities for Achievement (A) and Pleasure (P)

Daily Activity Schedule

DAY

TIME	ACTIVITY	A 0–10	P 0–10
8–9			
9–10			
10–11			
11–12			
12–1			
1–2			
2–3			
3–4			
4–5			
5–6			
6–7			
7–8			
8–9			
9–10			

DAY

TIME	ACTIVITY	A 0–10	P 0–10
8–9			
9–10			
10–11			
11–12			
12–1			
1–2			
2–3			
3–4			
4–5			
5–6			
6–7			
7–8			
8–9			
9–10			

NOTE: Grade activities for Achievement (A) and Pleasure (P)

How to Make Your Activity Schedule a Help Rather Than a Hindrance

1 *Be flexible.* Remember that the activity schedule is only a guide. Often things will happen that throw you off, such as an unexpected visitor, or something breaking down. Do not let this discourage you, just continue with your plan when you can. You will have to decide what to cut out of the planned activity, as now you will not be able to do everything you had planned.

2 *Think of alternatives.* Try to be prepared for things going wrong by having alternatives planned. You may have planned to go out for a walk and the weather changes, so have an alternative to substitute in its place. The unexpected does happen!

3 *Stick to the general plan.* If, for some reason, you are unable to do what you have planned at the time you planned it (you wanted to clean the bedroom and ended up talking to your son about his holiday plans), don't go back and try to do it later. Move on to the next activity, and plan to do what you missed the next day. If you finish an activity sooner than planned, leave your next activity until it is time for it on the schedule, and fill the gap with a pleasurable activity such as having a cup of tea, reading the newspaper, watching TV or phoning someone.

4 *Plan your activities by the hour or half-hour.* When planning activities, try not to be too specific or too vague. For example, cleaning the house is too vague, listing every piece of furniture would be too specific, but deciding to vacuum the living room would be about right. Also, remember to try to give yourself enough time. This may be longer than usual, as depression slows you down, so try to account for this as you plan your activities.

5 *Plan for quantity, not quality.* Write down the amount of time you are going to spend on a particular activity, not how much you are going to do in that time. How much you can do may depend on factors outside your control (interruptions, mechanical failures), or on other problems (difficulty in concentrating, fatigue). If you tell yourself you *must* weed the entire garden and you don't do it, you'll probably think of yourself as a failure and get discouraged. If you simply plan to weed for an hour, then how much you do is neither here nor there. Remember, *if a thing's worth doing, it's worth doing badly* – that is, doing something partially or to a lower standard than normal is better than doing nothing at all.

6 *Stick to the task in hand.* Try to stick to the schedule. It may not seem to help at first, but by sticking to it, it will eventually help you to overcome your depression. Don't expect too much, too soon, as you will only disappoint yourself.

7 *At the end of each planned day, review how you have done.* This will help you see how you did. It will help you see where you have been successful and where you have not. Both of these will help you to plan things better the next time. This may mean some changes in the structure of the day. If you had problems in sticking to the plan, ask yourself why this was.

8 *Remember that you are always doing something.* Sitting in a chair reading the paper is an activity. So is going to bed or staring out of the window brooding. But they may not be the activities that will give you the most satisfaction.

Practical Tasks

Depression often leads people to put off practical tasks they need to carry out. The pile mounts, and they end up feeling completely overwhelmed. Where to start?

You can help yourself get started on the tasks you need to do by following these steps:

1 Make a list of everything you have been putting off.

2 Number the tasks in order of priority – which needs to be done first? If you can't decide, number them in alphabetical order and work through them, or pick one that you expect to be easy. *The important thing at this stage is to do something.*

3 Take the first task and break it down into small steps. Think about each thing you have to do to complete the task.

4 Run through the task, step by step, in your mind. Write down any practical difficulties you think may occur, and work out how you will overcome them.

5 Write down any negative thoughts that come to you about doing the task, and answer them in the way shown in *Handout 5*. If you cannot overcome the negative thoughts at this stage, do not worry, as these will be tackled later on in therapy.

6 Try to work through the task step by step, dealing with difficulties and negative thoughts as they occur, just as you have practised.

7 If things are not going well, try to stick to the task until things start to get easier. It is best to stop when things are going well, as it will give you a sense of encouragement and make it easier to carry on next time.

8 As soon as you have finished a task, rate it at once for pleasure and achievement, and write this on your activity schedule.

9 Praise yourself for what you have done, and avoid thinking of the other things you still have to do. Your negative thoughts may tend to make you devalue what you have done, so be on the watch for this.

10 Take the next task, and tackle it in the same way.

Thought Blocks to Becoming More Active

If you have been depressed for some time, there are almost certainly negative thoughts that interfere with your ability to get on with things you need to do. You will learn how to overcome these depressed thoughts as you progress through this therapy. However, below are some common thoughts that interfere with people's ability to do things. There are also some possible alternative thoughts. These are not necessarily the right or only answers, just some suggestions to help you think about answers for yourself.

Negative Automatic Thoughts

I will never be able to do anything. There are always practical problems I can't overcome.

I can't keep a schedule – I've never been a record-keeper.

There's too much to do – I can't cope.

It's too difficult.

I don't want to.

I don't think I'm up to it just now – I'll wait till I'm feeling better.

Possible Answers

If I encounter practical difficulties, I could ask someone for help or advice. Most things in life have some degree of difficulty associated with them, and before I was depressed I usually managed.

Although I am not good at keeping records, I have at times used lists to help me with tasks such as shopping. Perhaps it is something I could learn, just as I have learnt skills in the past.

This is the depression talking. If I break down activities and do one piece at a time, then they won't seem so hard. I don't have to do everything now, I can do some things later.

It only seems difficult because I'm depressed. I've done more difficult tasks than this in the past.

What is important at the moment is not what I want to do, but what I need to do to make me feel better. Earlier, I did decide that this was what I was going to do, so I should get on and do it.

How do I know that I'm not up to it till I try? Doing it may make me feel better, and if I wait till I feel better it may never get done.

Thought Blocks to Becoming More Active

Negative Automatic Thoughts

It's too late to start now as I've already wasted too much time, and I'll just feel bad about it.

I can't decide what to do first.

There's no point in trying – I'll only make a mess of it, and then I'll feel worse.

I won't enjoy it.

I won't be able to do everything I've planned.

I'm not doing anything.

But I don't do anything worthwhile.

I don't deserve to enjoy myself.

I cleaned the car. So what?

Possible Answers

I'll feel even worse if I don't get on with it. I haven't really wasted time, I've just spent it on other things. However, now I need to get on with something different.

What is important at this stage is to do something. Once I do something, it will probably help me be clearer about what to do next.

How do I know until I try? Even if I make mistakes it doesn't mean that I'm a complete failure. I can learn from my mistakes.

How do I know? Since when have I been a fortune-teller? I need to try it and see.

So what? People often don't do all they plan. Doing something is better than nothing.

I need to write down what I do, and see. Maybe I just think I'm not doing anything.

I need to stop judging myself. It doesn't matter whether I think it is worthwhile doing – it will help me feel better.

Everyone deserves to enjoy themselves sometimes. I'm only feeling this way because I'm depressed.

Even though I can usually do this really easily, it took a lot of effort today. So I should be proud of myself for making the effort.

10 Hints to Help You Stick to the Plan

1 Set aside some time each evening to note what you have achieved, and what you plan to do the next day.

2 If you find something difficult, talk to yourself and give yourself instructions and encouragement. For example, if you plan to write a letter, say to yourself 'Go to the drawer and get a pen and paper.'; 'Write your address and the name of the person the letter is to', and so on. Praise yourself at each stage, for example, 'That's good', 'Well done'.

3 Watch out for unhelpful thoughts – try not to listen to them. Instead write them down to be answered in a more helpful way later, if necessary.

4 If you need to concentrate, remove any distractions – so turn off the TV, etc.

5 Avoid going to bed during the day. If you need to relax during the day, sit in a comfortable chair; have a bath; listen to music, or do anything else that helps you relax.

6 Give yourself little rewards as you go along – a cup of tea, a short rest, etc. You deserve a treat if you have worked hard.

7 Arrange reminders for yourself – for example, notes. Tell friends and family to help you keep your plan.

8 Plan something that you can easily achieve to start the day. This will get you off to a good start.

9 Balance the things you need to do with the things you want to do.

10 Think of things that have been rewarding and pleasurable in the past, before you were depressed – these are likely to be rewarding again.

Introduction
_____

Set agenda – *5 minutes*
_____

Review homework – *5 to 10 minutes*
_____

This week's task: Describe nature of Negative Automatic Thoughts – *20 minutes*
_____

Discuss common thinking errors using handout – *15 minutes*
_____

Review session – *5 to 10 minutes*
_____

Set homework – *5 to 10 minutes*
_____

Materials needed – *Handouts 1 and 2 from Step 4*, and further copies of *Handouts 1 or 2 from Step 3* as appropriate to enable the client to continue to monitor their activity
_____

Step 4 · Negative Automatic Thoughts

Introduction

This session will focus on teaching the client about negative automatic thoughts. You will need to help them to understand the nature of negative automatic thoughts and their role in depression. After you have done this, you will then focus on helping them learn about common thinking errors. Before you can move on to doing these things, you will have to set the agenda for the session and review the homework from the previous week. The session will end with a review of the session and the setting of homework.

Set agenda

Begin the session in the usual way, by agreeing the agenda for this week. It is important that the previous step has been fully understood and the client has made some progress in increasing their activity levels, especially if they had low levels. The increase should have helped with their mood, to some extent, although the mood elevations that occur with activity may not be sustained for any length of time. You may need to reassure the client about this.

If there has been little progress with increasing activity, it is best to repeat the previous step until there is some progress, and to try to identify why they have not made any progress. This may or may not take all of this session. If not, then you can use some of the session to commence this step.

Review homework from last week

Check how the homework assignment went. Note any difficulties, and if necessary spend time trying to overcome these. Sometimes it is enough to make a mental note of the difficulties experienced, and to deal with these in the context of future assignments or in-session tasks. If all went well, give positive feedback and move on to today's topic.

This week's task

If the client is ready to move on, then introduce the idea that this step will start to focus on their thinking style. It is likely that some of their thinking problems will already have become apparent from the previous steps. You should use this information in your description of negative automatic thoughts. Do so by describing the nature of negative automatic thoughts (see below), and then picking an appropriate example that you have identified from the previous sessions. Give them *Handout 1 for Step 4* to help them understand the nature of negative automatic thoughts.

Negative automatic thoughts

When people are depressed their thinking becomes very biased and negative. These negative thoughts appear spontaneously and frequently. They are called *negative automatic thoughts* and are usually focused on one of three areas:

1 *Themselves* – typical thoughts are 'I'm a loser', or 'I'm useless'. (Pick examples from the client's previous sessions.)

2 *Their world* – typical thoughts are 'No-one cares about me', or 'My job is lousy'.

3 *Their future* – typical thoughts are 'It will always be this way', or 'I'll never find any friends'.

Table 5 details the characteristics of negative automatic thoughts.

TABLE 5 · CHARACTERISTICS OF NEGATIVE AUTOMATIC THOUGHTS

Automatic: This means that they occur without any effort. They just pop into the client's mind – that is, they are the first thing that occurs to them. It's as if the thoughts are second nature to them.

Distorted: To anyone other than the client, they do not fit the facts. When challenged to think about their thoughts in a rational way, even the client will accept that they are distorted.

Unhelpful: The thoughts always lead the client to be more depressed, pessimistic and inactive. This means that they never help the client to achieve the goals that they desired when well.

Plausible: As the thoughts are not challenged by the client, even though they may seem silly to others, the client accepts them as true. As mentioned above, they seem like second nature to the client.

Involuntary: Even though the thoughts can be distressing, it can be very hard for the client to turn them off. Negative automatic thoughts seem to fill their mind, and thinking about more positive aspects of their life can be very difficult.

Persistent: They can be very hard to turn off, it takes a lot of effort.

Negative automatic thoughts lead to depression, and depression leads to more negative automatic thoughts. This sets up a vicious cycle and a downward spiral. The depression then becomes self-sustaining. This is why it is important to learn how to overcome these negative automatic thoughts. However, before the client can do this they have to understand a little more about the way they think.

Whenever something happens, individuals try to make sense of it – that is, to explain why it happened, what it means, and how to, and whether to, respond. They do this by comparing what has just happened with previous events of a similar nature. As mentioned earlier, the brain deals with large amounts of information collected as a result of our experiences, by developing rules about the way the world works. Everyone shares many of these rules – for example, hot things burn you and cause pain. These rules are in the main helpful. However, people also have more private rules that are not the same for each person. These rules for living, or beliefs, are also usually helpful, but sometimes they become unhelpful or dysfunctional. People who have dysfunctional beliefs are more likely to become depressed. These beliefs can often lie inactive for many years, waiting to be triggered by some event. Dysfunctional assumptions will be dealt with in detail later on, in Steps 7 and 8. When these dysfunctional beliefs are activated, negative automatic thoughts become more prominent and frequent, and this causes depression and the downward spiral mentioned earlier.

Using *Handout 2 for Step 4*, go through the common thinking errors and try to help the client identify which of these they commit. As you talk through these errors with the client, try to use examples that they have already talked about in previous sessions. The aim of this process is to help the client become more aware of their negative automatic thoughts. This will be the first stage of the cognitive approach to overcoming the client's depression.

Review the session

Review the session by asking the client what topics have been covered, and what they have learnt today, to ensure that they have understood what has been covered. If there are some areas that they have not understood, this can be noted and dealt with in the next session. Ask for feedback about your performance – for example: 'Did I explain things clearly enough?', 'Did I spend enough too much time on X or Y?'.

Set homework

Ask the client to continue the activity schedules. Ask them to read through the handout and to try to identify errors in their thinking so that they are prepared for the next session, which will focus more on identifying negative automatic thoughts and ultimately challenging them.

Characteristics of Negative Automatic Thoughts

Automatic. This means that they occur without any effort. They just pop into your mind. In other words, they are the first thing that occurs to you. It's as if the thoughts are second nature.

Distorted. To anyone other than the yourself, they do not fit the facts. When challenged to think about your thoughts in a rational way, even you may accept that they are distorted.

Unhelpful. The thoughts always lead you to be more depressed, pessimistic and inactive. This means that they never help you to achieve the goals that you desired when well.

Plausible. As the thoughts are not challenged by you, even though they may seem silly to others, you accept them as true. As mentioned above, they seem like second nature to you.

Involuntary. Even though the thoughts can be distressing, it can be very hard for you to turn them off. Negative automatic thoughts seem to fill your mind, and thinking about more positive aspects of your life can be very difficult.

Persistent. They can be very hard to turn off; it takes a lot of effort.

Common Thinking Errors

There are 10 thinking errors that are common in negative automatic thoughts and depressed people. Although non-depressed people may also make the thinking errors, theirs are neither so extreme nor so frequent. Read through the list below, and see which apply to you. You may not make all of them, but you are sure to recognise some.

1 *All-or-nothing thinking.* Everything is seen in terms of black and white, with no shades of grey. For instance, if you make a simple mistake, which anyone could make, you see it as a disaster.

2 *Over-generalisation.* If one thing is bad, then everything is bad. You often use 'always' and 'never'. You make an error and say things like 'I *always* get things wrong'.

3 *Mental filter.* Your mind only sees the negative side and never notices the positive, leading to the idea that life is one series of depressing events.

4 *Disqualifying the positive.* This is similar to the mental filter, but in this you notice a positive event and then undermine it by saying something such as 'Anyone can do that', or 'It was a lucky guess.' This allows you to maintain your negative beliefs, even though there is evidence to contradict them.

5 *Jumping to conclusions.* You make an assumption, with no evidence to support it. For instance, someone may not notice you in the street, and you assume they have fallen out with you or are angry with you, without checking this out. Or you may predict a negative outcome for something you plan to do, even though you have no evidence for this.

6 *Magnification or minimisation.* Making mountains out of molehills, or reducing the importance of positive information. For example, because you are late you think your friend will be angry and never want to see you again. Or, someone says you are really interesting and a good friend, and you think that they say that about everyone, or are only saying it to make you feel better.

7 *Emotional reasoning.* I feel it, therefore it must be true. You let your heart rule your head. So you might think because you feel guilty, you must have done something wrong.

8 *Shoulds, oughts and musts.* When you tell yourself you should, ought or must do something, and then fail or cannot do what you set out to do, you criticise yourself. You leave yourself no room for manoeuvre, and do not allow for the interference of external factors. If you direct the 'shoulds', 'oughts' and 'musts' at others, you get frustrated and angry when they don't come up with the goods, or use it as an example of your own undesirability.

9 *Labelling and mislabelling.* This is an extreme form of over-generalisation. You give yourself a label associated with a negative behaviour — for example, if you make a mistake, you describe yourself as hopeless. It is the event that goes wrong, but you label yourself, not the event.

10 *Personalisation.* You assume responsibility for everything that goes wrong, even when there is no evidence for it. So if the washing machine breaks, you might blame yourself for mistreating it, even though there is no evidence for this. You blame yourself, but in reality blame is only reasonable if you intend something, otherwise it is unfortunate and regrettable.

Step 5 · Quick Control of Negative Automatic Thoughts

Introduction

Set agenda – *5 minutes*

Review homework – *5 to 10 minutes*

This week's task: Describe ways of gaining quick control of negative automatic thoughts – *20 minutes*

Practise one or two methods of controlling negative automatic thoughts – *15 minutes*

Review session – *5 to 10 minutes*

Set homework – *5 to 10 minutes*

Materials needed – *Handouts 1 or 2 for Step 3* as appropriate, and *Handout 1 for Step 5*

Introduction

This session will focus on teaching the client about how to control negative automatic thoughts. You will need to describe to them the techniques listed below. After you have done this, you will then focus on helping them to practise these in the session, and decide which ones they think will be best for them. Before you can move on to doing these things, you will have to set the agenda for the session and review the homework from the previous week. The session will end with a review of the session and the setting of homework.

Set agenda

Begin the session in the usual way, by agreeing the agenda for this week. This will again include the familiar items — that is, reviewing the homework; tasks for today; review of the session, and setting the homework.

Review homework from last week

Check how the homework assignment went. Check that they have continued with their activity schedule, and that they understand the handout on thinking errors. If necessary, plan to spend some more time on these today. If all went well, give positive feedback and move on to today's topic.

This week's task

If the client is ready to move on, then introduce the idea that this step is about starting to focus on controlling their negative thoughts and associated depression. In this session you will describe some ways of quickly reducing the intensity of negative emotions and thoughts. These should only be used in the early stages of overcoming the client's depression, or when they feel overwhelmed by their feelings. They will give the client a sense of control, but they will not provide a long-term solution to their problems. However, at the beginning clients need some success quickly, even if this is only temporary. There is nothing like success to make clients feel better. The aim here is to help the client to escape their negative thoughts, and in later steps they will learn how to challenge them.

Explain to the client that they are learning new skills, therefore they should not expect immediate success. Tell them to try out different techniques, and use the ones most suited to them. Explain that they should try to use them whenever they feel bad. The client may find that one will work on one occasion, but not another. If this happens, they should be instructed to continue trying another until they find one that works. Because the client is depressed, they are likely to predict failure and therefore not try (remember the tendency to jump to conclusions from the previous step). Initially these techniques may only work for a few minutes, but with practice they will be effective for longer periods, and may eventually become second nature.

Begin by going through *Handout 1* with the client. First, describe the distraction techniques, and then go on to the ways of limiting the expression of sadness. After describing each technique, check with the client if they have understood it, and ask them for their thoughts on its usefulness for them. Do not expect all of the techniques to be useful. In fact, clients often use only two or three on a day-to-day basis. So, if they think that most of the techniques are not relevant to them, that is not a problem. Reassure them of this, and encourage them to use the ones they are most comfortable with.

Take your time over the explanations. If it is not possible to go through the whole handout, this is nothing to worry about as the client can read through them at home.

It may be helpful for you to demonstrate one of the techniques that the client has chosen. For example, if they have chosen to use the running commentary, talk about what you are doing — for example: 'I am sitting here in this room with a client, we are discussing ways of controlling negative feelings. I have just described various techniques that are often helpful. I am now running through an example of these with the client'.

After you have demonstrated a technique, ask the client to try it themselves. Make sure you have time to try out at least two techniques in the session. If the client is unable to implement one of the techniques they have chosen, then ask them to choose another and try again with that one. Sometimes a technique that initially seems easy for the client, can in fact be difficult. This is why it is helpful to practise the techniques within the session. If clients try for the first time at home and are unsuccessful, they will probably give up. If the client has difficulties with one of the techniques they choose, then this can be used as an example of how when one technique does not work for them they should try another.

Table 6 describes various distraction techniques. These are described in detail in *Handout 1 for Step 5*. Use this with the client to help them learn how to use them.

TABLE 6 · DISTRACTION TECHNIQUES

1 · Focusing on an object.

2 · Sensory awareness.

3 · Visualising pleasant scenes.

4 · Fantasies.

5 · Mental exercises.

6 · Running commentary.

Limiting the expression of sadness

Often it is helpful for the client to talk about their problems with their family and friends. However, sometimes it makes them more aware of their feelings, and increases their distress. It may also put strain upon relationships within the family and with friends, as they often feel unable to help the client. Therefore, it is often helpful for the client to be able to limit the amount of time they spend talking to others about how bad they feel. *Handout 1* includes several tips to help them avoid talking about their depression. Table 7 lists ways of limiting the expression of sadness.

TABLE 7 · LIMITING THE EXPRESSION OF SADNESS

1 · Emotional temperature-taking.

2 · Talking about positive or neutral events.

3 · Focusing attention on the other person.

Review the session

Ask the client to describe what they have learnt during the session, and for their thoughts about how useful they think it will be to them. If the client is too optimistic or too pessimistic, then you should try to get them to be more realistic in their aims. However, it is part of being depressed to be pessimistic, so do not worry too much about this. It is useful for the therapist to make a note of the client's expectations as they are often lower than their actual experience in the coming week, and this can be used to demonstrate how they underestimate themselves.

If the client has understood the session reasonably well, then it is time to move on to setting the homework. If there are some misunderstandings, try to correct these first.

Set homework

Instruct the client to read through the handout again, preferably the next day, and then start to use the techniques over the next week. Tell them to use the techniques whenever they experience a sudden worsening of their mood, or whenever they feel very depressed.

They should also be encouraged to keep up with the activity schedule, so you may need to provide more *Handouts 1 or 2 for Step 3.*

Check that the client has understood your instructions, and then end the session.

Quick Control of Negative Thoughts and Feelings

This handout will describe some ways of helping you to establish some control over your feelings of depression and negative thoughts. These are useful in the early stages of overcoming your depression, and can also be used at other times when your feelings overwhelm you. Having something that can give you control can make you feel more optimistic – there is nothing like success. These techniques often only work for brief periods; however, as you become more proficient in them you will start to be able to control your feelings for longer periods. They help by stopping the negative thoughts that lead to the symptoms of depression. However, they do not help to overcome the negative thoughts, and so do not provide a long-term solution. What they do is give you some temporary relief from your symptoms, and this can be very welcome at this stage in your problems.

Several different techniques are described. You should try them out and use the ones that most suit you. Remember, you are learning new skills, and therefore should not expect immediate success. You should try to use the techniques whenever you feel bad. You may find that one will work on one occasion, but not on another. If this happens, try another one until one works. Because you are depressed, you are likely to predict failure and therefore not try (remember jumping to conclusions, from the previous step). Initially, these techniques may only work for a few minutes, but with practice they will be effective for longer periods, and may eventually become second nature.

Focusing on an object

When you notice yourself feeling bad, choose an object in your surroundings and describe it to yourself in as much detail as you can. Anything will do – a chair, a house, a tree, a light switch. Ask yourself questions about it. What is it? What colour is it? What shape? Has it any flaws? How would you improve it? The more intensively you involve yourself in it, the better you are likely to feel.

Sensory awareness

Make yourself aware of your surroundings as a whole. Use as many senses as you can, as intensely as you can. What can you see? Hear? Feel? Smell? Taste? The more senses you use, the more effective the strategy will be. Try to immerse yourself in every detail, no matter how trivial.

Visualising pleasant scenes

Use memories of pleasurable experiences you have had, to distract yourself. Again, make the memories as vivid and detailed as you can. Where were you? Who with? What could you see? Hear? How did you feel?

Quick Control of Negative Thoughts and Feelings

Fantasies

Use your imagination to fantasise about things you would like to happen. What exactly would you do for instance, if you won £1 million? Or if you had the opportunity to travel the world, where would you go? What would you like to do and see? Who would you go with? Or try to imagine a time in the future when you will no longer be sad.

Mental exercises

These can be a useful way of distracting yourself from painful thoughts. For instance:

- Counting backwards from 100 in sevens (when you finish, start again at 105, then 110, and so on).
- Recalling what you heard on the news.
- Recalling what you would see on a journey or a walk familiar to you.
- Remembering poetry or songs you have learnt in the past.

Running commentary

Describe to yourself, in detail, what you are doing. For instance, if you get tense while driving, give yourself a running commentary on what you are doing: 'Now I'm changing up. I put my left foot on the clutch and press down, I move the gear lever. There is a car in front of me, its registration number is ... I'm keeping at a distance of x metres from it.'

Limiting the expression of sadness

Sometimes, talking to someone about your problems can be a great help. But it may only make you more painfully conscious of your feelings, and strain relationships with family and friends, who feel unable to be of real help to you. Try to limit the amount of time you spend talking to others about how bad you feel:

- Avoid emotional 'temperature-taking'. Don't introduce the subject of your depression yourself, and if asked how you feel, reply briefly and immediately change the subject by, for example , replying 'And how about you?'.
- Make a point of talking about positive or neutral events and experiences.
- Focus your attention on the other person. Think of questions to ask them, and make yourself concentrate on, and respond to, their replies.

Session 1

Introduction

Set agenda – *5 minutes*

Review homework – *5 to 10 minutes*

This week's task: Describe use of thought record – *30 to 40 minutes*

Review session – *5 to 10 minutes*

Set homework – *5 to 10 minutes*

Materials needed – One copy of *Handouts 1, 3 and 4*. Two or three copies of *Handout 2*

Session 2 onwards

Introduction

Set agenda – *5 minutes*

Review homework – *5 to 10 minutes*

This week's task: Use thought records to challenge negative automatic thoughts – *30 to 40 minutes*

Review session – *5 to 10 minutes*

Set homework – *5 to 10 minutes*

Materials needed – Several copies of *Handout 2*

Step 6 · Challenging Negative Automatic Thoughts

Session 1

Introduction

Step 6 will usually take several sessions of treatment. It involves the key component of the cognitive method. The client is taught how to challenge their negative automatic thoughts, and as they become more able to do this it lessens their depression.

The main task in the initial session is to help the client understand the nature of negative automatic thoughts, and then to demonstrate ways of recording them. The subsequent sessions in this step will focus on challenging negative automatic thoughts by reviewing the daily record sheets, looking at examples of negative automatic thoughts and the client's responses.

Set agenda

Begin the session in the usual way, by agreeing the agenda for this week. This will again include the usual things – reviewing the homework; tasks for the week; review of the session, and setting of homework.

Review homework from last week

Ask the client how they have managed with the quick control methods. Ensure that they have been able to use at least two of the methods with some success. If they have not been able to, you will have to set aside some time for this in today's session. The client needs to be able to use only two or three methods to control their depressed moods. They are used only when the mood is intense.

This week's task

According to the cognitive theory of depression, negative automatic thoughts are the main factor in maintaining a depressed mood. They form part of a vicious circle in which depressed mood, negative automatic thoughts and altered behaviours reinforce each other. That is, negative automatic thoughts lead to a depressed mood, which in turn leads to behavioural changes (often inactivity), which then lead to negative automatic thoughts. This circle can operate in either direction, as illustrated in Figure 5.

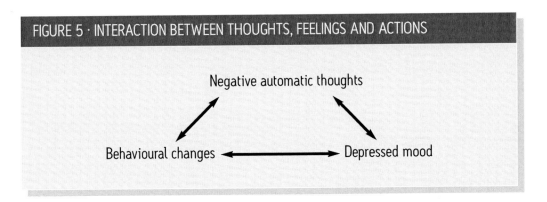

FIGURE 5 · INTERACTION BETWEEN THOUGHTS, FEELINGS AND ACTIONS

Negative automatic thoughts

Behavioural changes ⟷ Depressed mood

Table 5 described the characteristics of negative automatic thoughts. Remind the client of these characteristics, using *Handout 1 for Step 4.*

Handout 2 for Step 4 gives some examples of thinking errors, and *Handout 1 for Step 6* some alternative ways of thinking to overcome common thinking errors. Go through these with the client. Give them time to reflect on what you are saying, and ask them if they have any questions or thoughts about what you have told them.

Next, explain to the client that the first stage in challenging their negative automatic thoughts is to learn how to recognise when they are happening. To help them do this, ask them to keep a record of their thoughts on the Daily Thought Record Sheet *(Handout 2 for Step 6).*

Instruct the client to start recording their daily negative automatic thoughts on the sheets. The record sheet has seven sections. Tell the client to concentrate on only the first three sections over the next week. Every time they experience an intense mood they should fill in the sheet. In Section 1, they describe the situation in which the change in mood occurred. To help them do this, use the familiar 'Who?', 'What?', 'Why?', 'When?' form of question. For example, 'Who was I with?'; 'What was I doing just before the thought?'; 'Why was I doing that, or in that place?'; 'When did it occur?'.

In Section 2, they write about the moods they experienced. Instruct them to describe each mood in a single word. This is because extended explanations of moods often lead to a description of the situation, or of the negative automatic thoughts. To help the client become more clear about the role of negative automatic thoughts in generating their moods, their thoughts and moods need to be kept separate. Moods might be described as depressed, sad, irritated, hopeless, unreal, empty, and so on. The client is then instructed to rate the mood for its intensity. Zero per cent means that it is not present at all; 100 per cent means that it is as intense as the client could possibly imagine it to be.

In Section 3 the client should write down the negative automatic thoughts that they experienced. To help them to identify the thoughts, give them *Handout 3 for Step 6.* This contains questions that help them identify negative automatic thoughts.

Spend time going through this with the client, and work through an example with them. The client should try to put down the thoughts exactly as they experience them, word for word, if possible. Sometimes clients experience two conflicting thoughts, one of which is probably a gut feeling, the other a more rational idea. The gut feeling is more likely to be the negative automatic thought associated with the mood, and they should be instructed to record this in Section 3. It is useful to make a note of the rational thought, as this may be the way the client would think if they were not depressed.

In order to find a suitable example, try to get the client to recall the last time they felt very low, especially if it was associated with a sudden change in their mood. Ensure they have a pen or pencil, and get them to write down how they felt. It is best if the client does the writing. Start with writing down their mood, as the client usually finds this the easiest thing to identify. With the help of *Handout 3,* fill out Sections 1–3. As it is important to get as full a picture as possible, keep prompting the client, using the questions on *Handout 3.* Ask them, 'Was there anything else happening?'; 'Was anyone else present?'; 'What were you doing before?'; 'Were there any other thoughts going through your mind?'.

Sometimes the thoughts come not so much in verbal form as in the form of images. That is, the person has an internal picture of something happening. Prompt for these if they have not been able to produce any negative automatic thoughts. Suggest to them that the thoughts can come as images, like photos or movies in their mind. If they have experienced an image they should write this down in Section 3.

After each negative automatic thought, the client then rates their belief in it. They may have difficulty with this initially. It may seem a strange notion to them, as they may think that you either believe the thoughts or not. However, it is usually easy to persuade them that we all have grades of conviction in our thoughts. For example, we might think someone doesn't like us, but we're not sure, so may only be 50 or 70 per cent convinced of this.

They may have written down several negative automatic thoughts associated with a situation, or just one. Get them to rate their belief in all of them. The degree of conviction is likely to be high – between 70 and 100 per cent for most of them. If the degree of conviction is low, and the strength of the emotion is high, then it is likely that the client hasn't captured the important negative automatic thoughts. If this is the case, try exploring the negative automatic thoughts further.

You could use the downward arrow technique. In this, you write out the negative automatic thought at the top of the page, and below it draw a downward pointing arrow, then ask the client: 'If this is true, what does that mean about you, your world, your future?' Or you could say: 'What's so bad about that?' Then write down what they say, and then draw another arrow, and keep doing this till they can't go any further, or they reach a point at which anyone who believed the final thoughts would also feel very emotional. Diagram 6 illustrates this.

When they have reached the endpoint, check that the conclusions makes sense to them – that is, the final thought appears realistic to them. It important that it is the client's chain of thought that is captured. This technique is very useful when it comes to challenging negative automatic thoughts in the next session.

FIGURE 6 · DOWNWARD ARROW TECHNIQUE

My husband was angry with me.

What's so bad about that? What did it mean to you?

He probably does not like me any more.

If that were true, what does that mean for you?

He might leave me.

And if he did, what does that mean for you, or what would it lead to?

I'd be alone forever.

Instruct the client to record their negative automatic thoughts as soon as they happen. If possible, they should carry their Daily Thoughts Record Sheet with them to enable them to do this. Sometimes it may not be possible for them to write down their thoughts immediately. For example, they may be driving their car, or be in a meeting. If possible, they should jot down a few words, or rehearse what happened in their mind. They should then fill out the form as soon as possible afterwards. When they come to write down what happened, they should try to perform an action replay in their mind.

As the client starts to focus on their thoughts, they may start to feel worse. This is because they have been avoiding their negative automatic thoughts, possibly by using the distraction techniques learnt in Step 5. If they start to feel worse, they may find excuses to put off collecting their thoughts. For example, 'I'm too busy'; 'I'm feeling too bad today'; 'I'll start tomorrow'; 'This makes me feel worse and it won't help.' Warn the client about this, and emphasise the importance of not letting these thoughts get in their way; some may even be negative automatic thoughts. If they had similar problems when starting to become more active, but eventually gained some benefit from increased activity, remind them of this. You could use an analogy, such as how difficult it is when a person starts on a diet, or tries to stop smoking, or to get fit.

Because clients find it hard to complete the Daily Thought Record, it can seem like a test. It is important that you explain that they are not going to be judged in any way. This includes their success, or otherwise, in completing the form, or on any of the thoughts that they write down. So, even if they think that what they have written sounds stupid, or they are ashamed of their thoughts, it is important to let them know that it doesn't matter. Explain to the client that, rather than viewing it as a test, they should see it as acquiring a new skill. Learning new skills always requires practice, and people usually make mistakes at first. However, as the saying goes, practice makes perfect. Therefore, spending time each day practising will help them improve their skills in recognising their thinking patterns, and lead them to being able to make the changes that will help them overcome their difficulties.

Table 8 is an example of a Negative Automatic Thought Daily Record. As you can see, the client has produced a good description of the situation; has been able to identify the moods associated with the situation, and also produced some negative automatic thoughts associated with the situation.

TABLE 8 · DAILY THOUGHT RECORD (SECTIONS 1 TO 3)

1 · *Situation* (Describe the situation in as much detail as possible)	I was sitting at the dinner table with my family. My son didn't eat much of his meal, and quickly left the table without saying anything. My husband seemed to play around with his food rather than eat it. When I tried to talk to him, he ignored me.
2 · *Mood experienced* (Try to use a single word and then rate the severity of the mood from 0 to 100 per cent)	Depressed — 85 per cent Hopeless — 80 per cent
3 · *Automatic thoughts* (Describe what was going through your mind at the onset of the automatic thought. Rate how much you believe in the thought from 0 to 100 per cent)	1 My family does not care about me. — 70 per cent 2 I must be a drain on them. — 90 per cent 3 I have never been a good mother to my children. — 60 per cent 4 My husband would probably prefer to be with someone else. — 90 per cent

Review the session

Ask the client to tell you what they have learnt about negative automatic thoughts, and about filling in the thought record. Clarify any points as necessary. Check how they felt about this session, and their progress. This may generate some negative automatic thoughts. If it does, acknowledge this to the client, but do not try to deal with them now. Tell the client that the next session will be about overcoming their negative automatic thoughts.

Set homework

Remind the client that keeping up with their activity is important. At this stage they will probably still need to continue using the activity schedules, most likely the weekly schedule. Give them further copies if necessary.

This week's homework will be to fill out the Daily Thought Record Sheets (*Handout 2*), Sections 1–3 only. This should be done as often as possible. They will need at least one sheet per day, so it will probably be best to give them 10 sheets to take home.

Sessions 2, 3, 4, and so on
Introduction

The next few sessions will focus upon teaching the client how to challenge their negative automatic thoughts. They will need to continue to fill in the Daily Thought Record Sheets, and the sessions will focus on the contents of the sheets. The client will gradually learn ways of dealing with their negative automatic thoughts. This should lead to a significant improvement in their depressed mood. Throughout these sessions, you should use the Socratic dialogue as described in Part 1 of this book. During the sessions, you should start to notice themes within the client's thoughts. The negative automatic thoughts are often about similar themes. Try to identify what these themes are, as in Step 8 you can use these to identify the client's dysfunctional assumptions and help them to overcome these.

Set the agenda

Tell the client that the next few sessions will be devoted to helping them learn how to challenge their negative automatic thoughts. Explain that this will involve them continuing to fill out the Daily Thought Record Sheets. In this and subsequent sessions they will learn how to gather the evidence concerning their negative automatic thoughts, both supporting the thoughts and, more crucially, evidence that it is in contradiction to them. They will then be in a position to start developing alternative thoughts that will help them to overcome their depressed mood.

Review the homework from last week

Ask them if they had any difficulties in the last week, and how they got on with their homework. Assuming there have been no major difficulties, suggest to the client that the focus of today's session should be reviewing some of their Daily Thought Record Sheets. In the process of reviewing their thoughts, as captured on the sheets, you will then be able to help the client to learn how first to collect the evidence and then develop alternative thoughts.

If there have been any significant developments between the sessions, then it may be necessary to deal with these. However, hopefully they will have been recorded on the Daily Thought Record Sheets, so that this will not really lead to a deviation from the central task of learning how to overcome negative automatic thoughts.

This week's task

The client will have been keeping the Daily Thought Record Sheets for the last week. They should have filled out the first three columns. This means that they should have some data on the situations in which they have experienced emotional distress, and on the negative automatic thoughts associated with these mood changes.

With the client, choose one example from their record sheet. Try to choose one that will be easy to work on. This will often be one that is not that severe. If possible, also choose a situation from which it will be easy to gather evidence for and against the negative automatic thoughts. Thoughts that are about very specific things are usually easier to work on than those on more global issues. For example, 'My husband doesn't like me' is more specific than 'I don't think I'm a very likeable person.' However, sometimes one has to work on more global issues at the beginning, and if this is the case you will need to break them down into more specific components. Taking 'I don't think that I'm a very likeable person' as an example, you could ask the client to consider the evidence for this in relation to just one person they know well. Then you could pick another person, and then groups of people, such as work colleagues.

Sometimes a client will want to choose a more complex topic to work on. Discuss the difficulties of this with the client, and their reason for choosing this topic. If they still want to continue, then work with their choice. They will either be successful, or they will have difficulty and be more likely to work on something less difficult next time. If they do fail, reassure them that it was not surprising that they could not challenge such difficult thoughts. It is a skill they have to learn, and it is usually best to start on easier things.

When you have chosen a negative automatic thought to work on, then ensure that the client has the Daily Thought Record in front of them and a pen to write with. Ask the client to write down any evidence that supported their negative automatic thought in *Section 4 of Handout 2*. Clients will not usually have much difficulty with this. They are encouraged to think of all the evidence that supports their negative automatic thought. When they have done this, they move on to the next section, concerning evidence that does not support their negative automatic thought or is against their thought. This may prove more difficult for them to do, especially if the mood they experienced was very strong.

Here are various ways of helping the client identify evidence to challenge their negative automatic thoughts:
- Examining the client's thinking style
- Using Socratic dialogue and the downward arrow technique
- Using *Handouts 3 and 4*.

In *Handout 2 for Step 4*, common thinking errors were described. These are often the cause of the client's negative automatic thoughts, so check through these with them to see if these thinking errors distort their thoughts. *Handout 1* in this step relates to this. You can use it to illustrate some of these common errors in thinking.

You will often find that clients do not make the whole range of thinking errors, only certain selected ones that they seem to commit almost habitually. If you identify that this is the case, then it will be necessary to focus on these with the client so that they become fully aware of when they are falling into particular thinking errors, and can develop ways of overcoming them. They may make these thinking errors even when not depressed, possibly in a less extreme way. They may act as 'seeds' for future episodes of depression.

In the first session of Step 6, the downward arrow technique was described, and this can be very useful in helping the client to identify evidence. It helps to take them through their chain of thinking. This often leads to other related thoughts and experiences that contradict the negative automatic thoughts. When the downward arrow technique is being used, the extremeness of some of their thinking is exposed and can be used to identify clear contradictions in their thoughts.

Handout 4 has a series of questions that clients can ask themselves about the situation in which they find themselves. These are designed to help them to think in alternative ways about the situation. They are self explanatory, and need no further explanation here. Use the handout with the client in the session.

For the client to be successful in challenging their negative automatic thoughts, they will have to muster significant evidence against them. Alternatively, the evidence that is contrary to the negative automatic thought needs to be so powerful that it outweighs all of the evidence supporting the negative automatic thought.

After the client has completed Sections 4 and 5 of the Daily Thought Record, they now need to develop alternative thoughts that are more balanced. The alternative thoughts may not be an absolute reflection of the truth, as most other people would see it. The aim is to help the client to develop ways of thinking that are less likely to lead to a depressed mood, and that are sustainable in everyday life. You and they are *not* looking for ultimate truth, whatever that is.

To help the client to arrive at balanced thoughts, ask them to review all of the evidence for and against a negative thought. Then help them to write one sentence that summarises all of the evidence for the negative automatic thought, and one sentence that summarises all of the evidence against it. Ask the client to join the two sentences with an 'and' to see if this is in fact a balanced belief. The two sentences may need to be further refined in some way. This can be done by further discussion and Socratic dialogue. As it is important for the client to fully embrace this new belief, you should avoid putting words into their mouth. If you need to make suggestions, rather than asking clarifying questions try to find something they have said in a previous session that relates to the negative thought but brings more balance to it.

The client writes this balanced thought in Section 6, and then in Section 7 rates how strongly they believe in this new alternative way of thinking. It is unlikely that they will believe it completely, but as time goes by they will start to gain greater conviction in their new ways of thinking. However, you should aim to have at least 60 per cent conviction in the new thought, if possible. If this is not the case, try to look for more evidence to overcome the negative automatic thought, or a different alternative one. In very depressed people this may still not be possible, so you will just have to accept their level of conviction and hope that with time this will strengthen.

Using the above methods, work through one to three negative automatic thoughts in each session with the client. As the sessions pass they will gradually get more proficient at challenging their negative automatic thoughts, and this will raise their mood.

Sometimes clients will not be able to find sufficient evidence to counteract their negative automatic thought. It is then necessary that they conduct their own research, or experiment to collect further evidence. Helping them do this is the focus of the next step.

In the example in Table 9, the client listed several pieces of evidence for her negative automatic thoughts. The last point – 'My husband doesn't seem interested in me' – is rather vague. This is often the case. Follow through by asking the client to give an example. In this case, the client went on to say that her husband was not as affectionate as he used to be; he gave her less cuddles, and so on.

TABLE 9 · DAILY THOUGHT RECORD (SECTIONS 4 TO 7)	
4 · *Evidence for the automatic thought*	1 My husband forgot our anniversary last month. 2 He only seems interested in his friends. 3 My husband doesn't seem interested in me.
5 · *Evidence that is against the automatic thought*	1 He had the opportunity to go away on a business trip, but said that he preferred to stay at home. 2 He arranged a surprise night out for me on my birthday. 3 He stopped hugging me after I got upset and told him to stay away from me. Despite this, he still touches me from time to time in an affectionate manner.
6 · *Alternative balanced thought* (Write out a sentence containing the balanced thought and rate your belief in it from 0 to100)	Although I think that my husband would be better off without me and doesn't care for me, I have no evidence for this. He is doing what I asked him to do by not cuddling me. Perhaps he's doing this as he thinks that is what I really want at present. <div align="right">60 per cent</div>
7 · *Re-rate your original mood from Section 2* (0 to100 per cent)	Depressed 50 per cent Hopeless 50 per cent

Now ask the client to identify evidence against the negative automatic thoughts. Again, deal with one thought at a time. In this example, the client was helped to identify the evidence against the negative automatic thought that her husband would rather be with someone else by the therapist asking a series of questions:

THERAPIST   Is there any reason that makes you think your husband does not want to be with someone else?

CLIENT   I'm not sure, but last month he was invited on a business trip away and he decided not to go.

THERAPIST	Do you know why not?
CLIENT	Not really, but be said he preferred to be at home.
THERAPIST	And you're at home, so he must want to be with you, at least some of the time.
CLIENT	I suppose so.
THERAPIST	Is there any other thing that would be against the idea that he would rather be with someone else?
CLIENT	I can't think of anything [long pause]. He did arrange a surprise birthday party for me.
THERAPIST	Do you think that he would have done this if he didn't want to be with you?
CLIENT	Probably not, but he might just have been doing it to please me.
THERAPIST	Does he often do things to please you?
CLIENT	[after pausing to think] Yes, I suppose he does.
THERAPIST	So, he often wants to please you?
CLIENT	Yes.
THERAPIST	Do you think that he would want to please you often, if he didn't want to be with you?
CLIENT	I suppose not.
THERAPIST	So, arranging a surprise party could be seen as evidence against your negative automatic thought. Perhaps you should write that down. Is there any other evidence against the negative automatic thought?
CLIENT	I can't think of anything at present.
THERAPIST	Why do think that your husband isn't affectionate to you?
CLIENT	Well, I'm not that affectionate to him.
THERAPIST	Has it always been like this?
CLIENT	No.
THERAPIST	[after a pause to allow the client to expand] When did things change?
CLIENT	I'm not certain, but about four months ago.
THERAPIST	Isn't that about the time you became depressed?
CLIENT	Yes. I found it hard to have my husband come near me, as I was thinking that he didn't want to be with me.
THERAPIST	So how did you respond to this?
CLIENT	I asked him not to touch me.
THERAPIST	You asked him not to touch you?
CLIENT	You know what I mean; not be affectionate.
THERAPIST	Did he accept this?
CLIENT	Yes and no. He said it upset him that I didn't want him to be affectionate, but if it would help he would try.

THERAPIST   So it was your decision to reduce the display of affection between you and your husband, and he reluctantly agreed out of his concern for you. Do you think that may be an indication that he cares for you and wants to be with you?

CLIENT   I suppose so. Shall I write that down also?

THERAPIST   What do you think?

CLIENT   Yes.

The client's depressed mood may not alter all that much at first. This may be because these first negative automatic thoughts you work on are not the ones that are driving the client's mood. Note which negative automatic thoughts have the most impact on the client's mood, as this will be helpful in identifying their dysfunctional assumptions later in therapy. Any small reduction in mood should be highlighted at the beginning, as it is evidence for the effectiveness of the model and also the method.

Examples of Thinking Errors Common in Depression

Thinking errors	Automatic thought	Possible answer
The fact that I believe something to be true does not necessarily mean that it is. Would other people accept my thought? What evidence do I have to back it up, or to contradict it? Am I confusing a thought with a fact?	When I met Peter in the street today, he didn't smile at me. I must have done something to offend him.	It's true that he didn't smile at me, but I have no reason to believe he's offended by me. It probably had nothing at all to do with me – maybe he just had something on his mind.
Am I jumping to conclusions? When people are depressed they often assume that people are thinking badly of them. However, I can never really know what people are thinking. I will try not to jump to conclusions about people's actions.	My husband suggested that we go out for a meal. He obviously can't stand my cooking.	I don't really know if that is true. He says that he wanted to help by reducing the pressure on me. Also, he often tells people I'm a good cook.
Am I assuming that my view of things is the only one possible? How would I have looked at this situation before I got depressed? How would another person look at it? How would I look at it if someone else described it to me?	At work today I really screwed up. I never get anything right.	If I wasn't depressed, I'd probably not be so bothered about it. Other people have made similar mistakes, and they haven't been criticised.
What do I want out of life? Is the way I am thinking now helping me to achieve this? Or is it standing in the way of what I want?	I've wasted so much of my life so much in the past.	Thinking about the past only makes me depressed. What I need to do is think about how I'm going to change my future.

Examples of Thinking Errors Common in Depression

Thinking errors	Automatic thought	Possible answer
What are the advantages and disadvantages of thinking this way? Many distorted thought patterns do have some advantages – that is what keeps them going. But do the disadvantages outweigh the advantages? I will try to find new ways of thinking in which the advantages outweigh the disadvantages.	I really must get on with everyone at work. Advantages – I will try hard to please people, and then they are more likely to like me. Disadvantages – I might not be able to please everyone, and then someone would not like me or be upset with me. That would be terrible.	Telling myself that I must get on with everyone is unrealistic, and just puts me under pressure and makes me anxious. It is impossible for everyone to like me all the time. It's very nice when they do, but if they don't, it's not the end of the world.
Am I asking questions that have no answers? Questions like 'Why am I like this?', 'How can I change the past?', 'Why is life so unfair?'. Brooding over questions like these is a guaranteed way to depress me.	When will I be better again?	When I keep thinking about this, it just makes me worse. I should focus on what I can do to overcome my depression.
Am I thinking in all-or-nothing terms?	I did that really badly.	The fact is, I didn't do it as well as I wanted to. That doesn't mean it was no good at all. I can't expect to do everything 100 per cent right.
Am I using ultimatum words in my thinking? I will try to watch out for words like always, never, everyone, nothing. The chances are that the situation is actually less clear-cut than that. Mostly it's a case of sometimes, some people and some things.	Everything always goes badly for me.	That's an exaggeration. Some things go badly for me, just like they do for anyone else, but some things go well.

Examples of Thinking Errors Common in Depression

Thinking errors	Automatic thought	Possible answer
Am I condemning myself as a total person on the basis of a single event? Depressed people often take difficulties to mean that they have no value at all as a person. Am I making this kind of blanket judgement?	I was so irritable with the children this morning. I am a terrible mother and a wicked person.	The fact that on a particular day, at a particular time, in particular circumstances, I was irritable, does not mean I'm a terrible mother or a wicked person. I can't reasonably expect never to be irritable. Making myself depressed by writing myself off completely is not going to help me to be nicer to the children when they get in from school.
Am I concentrating on my weakness and forgetting my strengths? How have I coped with similar difficulties in the past?	I can't stand being alone, now that Jane has gone.	I was alone before I met her. I made an effort to get out and meet people, and spent time doing things I enjoyed. In fact, I was quite happy – and probably can be again. I'll phone Bob for a start.
Am I blaming myself for something that is not really my fault? Depression is a difficult problem to solve, and blaming myself for it will only make me more depressed.	I must really be stupid to have these distorted thoughts.	Stupidity is one possible reason. When I look at myself as a whole, there's not much evidence that I'm stupid. I have these thoughts because I'm depressed. When I'm feeling better, I think quite differently.
Am I taking something personally which has little or nothing to do with me? In fact, it may have nothing to do with me.	Mary doesn't like me at all. She would never have shouted at me like that if she did.	I'm not the only person Mary shouts at. She's always on edge when things aren't going well for her, and she shouts at whoever is around. I've seen her. She'll get over it and probably apologise.

Examples of Thinking Errors Common in Depression

Thinking errors	Automatic thought	Possible answer
Am I expecting myself to be perfect? It is simply not possible to get everything right all the time. Accepting that I can't be perfect does not mean I have to give up trying to do things well. It means that I can learn from my difficulties and mistakes, instead of being upset and paralysed by them.	This is not good enough. I should have completed everything I planned to do.	I can't always expect to carry out everything I plan. I'm not God. I'm fallible, like any other human being. It would have been nice if I had finished, but the fact that I haven't is not a disaster. I should focus on what I have done, not on what I have failed to do. That way I will be encouraged to try again.
Am I using double standards? I may be expecting more of myself than I would of another person. How would I react to someone else in my situation? Would I be so hard on them? I can afford to be kind to myself as I would to someone else. It won't lead to collapse.	I'm pathetic. I shouldn't be so upset by things.	If someone else was upset by this situation, I'd be sympathetic towards them, and help them try to find a solution to the problem. I certainly wouldn't call them pathetic — I'd be able to see that that wouldn't help. I can do the same for myself. It will give me the courage to carry on.
Am I paying attention only to the black side of things? Am I, for instance, focusing on everything that has gone wrong during the day, and forgetting or discounting things I have enjoyed or achieved?	That was really a terrible day.	Hang on a moment. I was late for a meeting, and I had a disagreement with my son, but on the whole my work went well, and I enjoyed the cinema this evening. It wasn't a bad day. Remembering only the bad things is part of depression — watch out for it.

Examples of Thinking Errors Common in Depression

Thinking errors	Automatic thought	Possible answer
Am I overestimating the chances of disaster? How likely is it that what I expect will really happen? Is there really nothing I can do to change the course of events?	I didn't get all my work done today again. I'll get the sack.	When was the last time they sacked someone from this firm for not having time to finish a job? It's perfectly normal not to finish, when we all have to work under such pressure. If my boss comments, I can explain the situation to him.
Am I exaggerating the importance of events? What difference does a particular event really make to my life? What will I make of it in a week, a year, 10 years? Will anyone else remember what I see as a terrible thing today? If I do, will I feel the same way about it? Probably not.	I made a real fool of myself at that party. I'll never be able to face them again.	Don't make a mountain out of a molehill. Most people didn't even notice. I don't suppose anyone who did thought anything much of it. We'll probably laugh at it in the future – it certainly makes a good story.
Am I fretting about the way things ought to be, instead of accepting and dealing with them as they are? Am I allowing events in the world at large to feed my depression? Telling myself life is unjust, and people are brutes? It is sad that there is so much suffering in the world, and I may decide to do what I can to change things, but getting depressed about it does nothing to help.	That programme about old people in the slum was awful. Things should be different.	Things are as they are, and to want them different is counter to reality – like wishing the zebra had no stripes. Getting depressed about it is not going to help the situation. Why not see if I can visit someone at the old people's home down the road?

Examples of Thinking Errors Common in Depression

Thinking errors	Automatic thought	Possible answer
Am I assuming I can do nothing to change my situation? Pessimism about the chances of changing things is central to depression. It makes me give up before I start. I can't know that there is no solution to my problem until I try. Is the way I am thinking helping me to find answers, or is it making me turn down possible solutions without even trying them?	It's no good. I'll never sort this out.	If I tell myself that, I certainly won't. I will sit down and work out what I could do. Even if some of my solutions haven't worked before, that does not mean they won't work now. What was it that stopped them from working?
Am I predicting the future instead of experimenting with it? The fact that I have acted in a certain way in the past does not mean I have to do so in the future. If I predict the future, instead of trying something different, am I cutting myself off from the chance of change. Change may be difficult, but it is not impossible.	I'll never manage to stand up for myself. I never have.	The fact that I never have, does not mean I never can. Doing so will make me feel uncomfortable, but if I stick with it, it will become more natural. Also, other people will respect me more.

Daily Thought Record

1 · *Situation* (Describe the situation in as much detail as possible.)

_____

2 · *Mood experienced* (Try to use a single word, and then rate the severity of the mood from 0 to 100 per cent.)

_____

3 · *Automatic thoughts* (Describe what was going through your mind at the onset of the automatic thought. Rate how much you believe in the thought from 0 to 100 per cent.)

_____

4 · *Evidence for the automatic thought*

_____

5 · *Evidence that is against the automatic thought*

_____

6 · *Alternative balanced thought*
   (Write out a sentence containing the balanced thought, and rate your belief in it from 0 to 100 per cent.)

_____

7 · *Re-rate your original mood from Section 2* (from 0 to 100 per cent).

Speechmark ⑤ ℗

Questions to Help Identify Negative Automatic Thoughts

● What was going through my mind just before I started to feel this way?

● What was I doing, and what was going on around me?

● If this thought is true, what does it mean about me?

● What does this tell me about my life, or what the future will bring?

● What do I think might happen to make me feel this way?

● If this is true, what might it mean about the way other people think of me?

● What does it mean about other people in general?

● What recollections from the past are associated with this?

Questions to Help Find Evidence that Contradicts my Negative Automatic Thought

- Is there anything that shows that this thought is not completely true at all times?

- If my best friend or someone I loved had this thought, what would I say to them? If my best friend or someone who loves me knew I was thinking this thought, what would they say to me? What would they say to me that would cast doubt on my thoughts?

- Would I think about this kind of situation any differently if I was not feeling depressed?

- When I have felt this way in the past, what did I think about that helped me feel better?

- When I have been in similar situations before, what have I done to overcome them, and how did I cope?

- Is there anything at all that contradicts my thoughts, no matter how small?

- If I look back at this situation in four or five years from now, what will I make of it? Would it seem so important or difficult?

- Do I have strengths or capabilities that I am underestimating, that would help me overcome this situation?

- Is there anything in Sections 3 and 4 of the Daily Thought Record that is not supported by the evidence? In other words, am I jumping to conclusions?

- Am I being unreasonable and taking responsibility for something I have no responsibility for, or that was completely out of my control?

Introduction

Set agenda – *5 minutes*

Review homework – *5 to 10 minutes*

This week's task: Describe use of behavioural experiments – *30 to 40 minutes*

Review session – *5 to 10 minutes*

Set homework – *5 to 10 minutes*

Materials needed – One copy of *Handout 1*, two or three copies of *Handout 2*

Introduction

Challenging negative automatic thoughts may not be enough by itself to convince the client that the thoughts are incorrect. In order for new ideas to take root, they need to be backed up with real evidence. As the client has not thought in these ways in the past, they need to try out their new ideas. This allows them to check whether the new ways of thinking are, in fact, in line with reality. Also, the client may have developed ideas that are not quite appropriate and may need refining. The client's new beliefs will only take root if they constantly practise behaving according to them. In order to help the client, this step will be about teaching them to conduct what are called behavioural experiments.

Set agenda

Begin the session in the usual way, by agreeing the agenda for this week. This will include the usual things – reviewing homework, tasks for today (behavioural experiments), review of the session, and setting the homework.

Review homework from last week

Check how the client coped with last week's homework. This would probably have been keeping their Daily Thought Record. At this stage, they should be becoming fairly proficient at challenging their negative thoughts in at least some areas.

Over the previous weeks they may have been trying to deal with negative automatic thoughts that needed a behavioural experiment to help them overcome them. If one has occurred in the previous week then this can be used in today's session.

Deal with any simple problems that have occurred in the homework, then move on to the current task. If there were major problems, then they may have to be dealt with now, rather than moving on to behavioural experiments (unless using behavioural experiments is an effective way of dealing with them).

This week's task

We are all like scientists. We make predictions: 'If I press the bell, the bus will stop'; 'People don't like to be contradicted'; 'If I stand in the rain, I will get wet', and we act on them. We use information from our experiences to confirm or change our predictions. A depressed client is like a scientist gone wrong. He distorts experience to fit his negative beliefs, instead of using it to prove or change them.

Many negative thoughts take the form of predictions: 'I won't be able to do it'; 'Everyone will despise me'; 'If I say what I think, I will be rejected.' Because of these negative predictions, the client often avoids situations or trying things out. The aim of behavioural experiments is to get the client to review the evidence, look for alternatives, and take action to test them out. It should be as if the client were a scientist running an experiment to examine a new theory or hypothesis.

The steps involved are shown in Table 10. Tables 11 and 12 show two examples of the behavioural experiment in action.

TABLE 10 · HOW TO CONDUCT A BEHAVIOURAL EXPERIMENT

1 · The client is instructed to state their (negative thought) prediction clearly.

2 · They then have to review the evidence for and against it.

3 · Next, they decide on a plan of action that will test the truth of their prediction – an experiment.

4 · They then need to examine their results.

5 · If their prediction is not borne out (ie, their negative thought is shown to be false), so much the better – they have demonstrated a positive alternative in action.

6 · If their prediction is borne out (the negative thought is shown to be correct), then all is not lost, as this is also valuable information. What were they doing to bring about this result? Can they work out ways of acting and thinking differently in future, so as to bring about a more positive result? Once they have done so, they should then set up another experiment.

7 · What conclusions can they draw from their results?

TABLE 11 · EXAMPLE OF BEHAVIOURAL EXPERIMENTS

Example 1
Phil is studying Geology. He is afraid of asking questions in class as he thinks that he will look silly.

1 · *Prediction.* If I ask questions, then people will think I'm stupid.

2 · *Review of evidence.* If I was stupid, I wouldn't be in this class in the first place. Not knowing all the facts is not the same as stupidity. At this stage in the course, there are bound to be many things I don't know. I don't think other people are stupid because they ask questions. I have no evidence that other people think it's stupid to ask questions – in fact, the lecturer encourages questions. Asking questions is the best way to learn.

3 · *Experiment 1.* Over the next week, observe what questions are asked and what reactions they get.

4 · *Results.* Lots of questions were asked with no bad reactions that I could see. Several questions led to stimulating discussions. In fact, some of the questions I had thought about asking myself, but never had the nerve to do so. Sally asked a couple of questions with obvious answers. Some people laughed, but it didn't seem to upset her and nobody teased her.

5 · *Conclusion.* It's unlikely that anyone will think I'm stupid for asking questions, even if the answers are obvious. If some people do laugh it doesn't mean that they think I'm stupid.

Experiment 2. Ask a question in the next class. I can prepare for this by reading through these notes.

Use some of the material from the previous sessions to set up a behavioural experiment with the client. This will focus on a negative automatic thought that they have already identified. Usually, the negative automatic thought that you choose would have been difficult to deal with by verbal challenging alone. Choose something that is easy to do. Often, the thoughts that clients want to test out are quite complex things, which require sophisticated experiments. Try to avoid these at the beginning. Try to get them to work on a problem that they are likely to have a lot of success with. These can usually be identified by the extremeness of the negative automatic thought. The more extreme the thought, the less likely it is that the client's prediction will be accurate.

TABLE 12 · EXAMPLE OF BEHAVIOURAL EXPERIMENTS

Example 2
Sarah has been invited to a party. The thought of it fills her with panic. She is convinced that she will have nothing to say to anyone, and will not enjoy herself. This depressed her, as she thinks that she will lose all of her friends.

1 · *Prediction.* If I go, I will not be able to talk to anyone. I will have a bad time and lose all my friends.

2 · *Review of evidence.* Before I got depressed, I used to enjoy parties. It's true that since I became depressed I haven't got much pleasure out of most of them. Still, there have been one or two I enjoyed. Only people that I know well will be at this party. They know how I've been and won't expect a lot of me. If I don't go, I will miss the opportunity of enjoying myself, which will make me feel better if it works out.

3 · *Experiment 1.* Go to the party and see what happens. I can use distraction techniques to try to help me feel relaxed. I'll start by just listening to my closest friends, and then try to join in the conversation.

4 · *Results.* I went to the party, but did not enjoy it and left early. Why? I spent the whole evening thinking how happy everyone looked except for me. I was so busy thinking about myself, I couldn't concentrate on anything that was going on.

5 · *Conclusion.* My prediction was correct, but mainly because I was so preoccupied with negative thoughts. Despite this, two friends rang today, so one bad evening does not mean I'll completely lose contact.

Experiment 2. Next time, I will work harder at answering negative thoughts beforehand and distracting myself during the party. I will practise distraction exercises in the coming week.

You also need to take into consideration the social environment in which the client lives. For example, it would be inappropriate to test out beliefs concerning being inadequate with their spouse, if the spouse is critical. You need to bear in mind that the client may have chosen their partner because the partner reinforces the client's underlying dysfunctional attitudes. Family members can sometimes be problematic because they have shared the environment the client grew up in, and they may have similar dysfunctional beliefs.

The client should be instructed to use all the skills they have learnt in the previous steps to help them to change their way of behaving. You may be able to work through a behavioural experiment to its completion in the session, but usually you will only be able to discuss it and set it up for the client to do in between the sessions as homework.

Clients always find it difficult when they try out new ways of behaving. They feel uncomfortable; sometimes it feels to them as if they are deceiving people around them. You need to encourage them to persevere with their new ways of doing things. They may get a lot of help from people close to them, but this is not always the case. Sometimes their new behaviours are not to the liking of those around them. For example, if the client was afraid to stand up for themselves at work or in their relationship, and they try to act differently the people around them may not wish this to happen. When this is the case, you need to be especially supportive of their efforts. You will need to discuss the reasons why some people are critical, and look at the longer-term benefits of their new ways of being.

The client needs to identify the negative automatic thought they intend to challenge. You and the client then review the evidence for and against the thought. From this, the client is helped to find an alternative way of behaving, as in the examples given. Then, using *Handout 2 for Step 7,* help the client to decide how they are going to test the thought. Together you need to explore what may get in the way. You need to talk through the experiment and, at each point of their plan, ask them if they can identify obstacles. Often, they may not be particularly good at this task, and you may identify possible difficulties that they do not. If this is the case, try using Socratic dialogue to help them see potential problems. Once you identify any difficulties, you need to develop an action plan to overcome them. As you do this, get the client to write down the plan of action, potential difficulties, and the solutions you and they have identified.

When you and the client have finally worked through the plan of action, you need to decide together exactly when they are going to carry it out. As it will be difficult for the client, they often tend to put it off. By identifying a definite time to carry out the experiment, it becomes easier for the client to undertake it. Unless the client has a definite timetable, they often find excuses for delay.

After the client has a written plan of action, a timetable for implementing it, and carried it out, they will need to review the outcome. Initially you will have to go through the client's behavioural experiment with them. However, with time they should be able to review their own experiments; work out if or why they have been unsuccessful, and if necessary revise them for themselves.

If the experiment is successful, you should ask the client what they have learnt from it. Sometimes clients still distort the evidence that they have identified within an experiment. For example, if they have been more assertive at work and it proved effective, they may say that it was only because the boss was in a good mood. You will need to try to challenge this with them. However, if this proves unsuccessful, then the way to overcome this difficulty is to get them to repeat the experiment several more times. As they repeat the experiment over and over again, the weight of evidence eventually becomes so great that it is hard to ignore. In addition to this, the new way of behaving becomes less alien to them and they find it easier to do.

If the client's experiment is unsuccessful, you need to go over it with them and try to help them refine it if necessary. Usually, they have been unsuccessful because they have not followed their plan, as in Example 2. Spend time with the client looking at the reasons they did not follow their plan, and try to identify factors that could get in the way in the future. Discuss it with them, and identify means of overcoming obstacles.

If, however, they followed their plan and it still did not work out, get them to look at their prediction again. Was it too ambitious? Have they missed out some important information when setting up the experiment? Often, the failed experiment brings new information to add to the equation. It may illuminate some deficiencies in social skills, or another set of beliefs the client had not previously talked about. These can be tackled either by using the skills learnt in the last step, or by a further behavioural experiment.

Very occasionally, it is not possible to identify the reasons for failure. If this is the case, and you and the client cannot see any other way of dealing with it, then you need to encourage the client to work on another problem that they can solve. Praise them for trying hard, and reassure them that all is not lost. Let them know that by working on other issues they can still do something positive, and that they may be able to come back to this particular problem later. In these circumstances, the reason for failure may be because the problem is part of a larger issue, and a product of a dysfunctional assumption that is predominant in the client's belief system. At this stage they may not be strong enough, or have developed their skills sufficiently, to work on these. Dealing with dysfunctional assumptions is dealt with in the next step.

Review the session

As usual, check with the client that they understood what has been discussed this session, by asking them to review it for you. Check that they are happy with performing their own behavioural experiments.

Set homework

After working through an example with the client, ask them to test it out over the coming week. They may be able to perform more than one experiment each week. If this is the case, then encourage them to do so.

How to Conduct a Behavioural Experiment

1 State your prediction clearly (this is your negative thought).

2 Review the existing evidence for it and against it.

3 Decide on a plan of action that will test the truth of your prediction — an experiment.

4 Examine the results.

5 Draw conclusions from your results.

● If your prediction is not borne out (your negative thought is shown to be false), so much the better — you have demonstrated a positive alternative in action.

● If your prediction is borne out (the negative thought is shown to be correct), then all is not lost, as this is also valuable information. What were you doing to bring about this result? Can you work out ways of acting and thinking differently in the future, so as to bring about a more positive result? Once you have done so, you should then set up another experiment.

Record Sheet for Behavioural Experiments

1 · Describe the actions to be taken.

2 · Predict what will happen if the new belief is true. This includes both the initial emotional responses and the later outcome.

3 · Describe the possible things that could get in the way.

4 · Describe strategies to overcome these obstacles.

5 · Record the result of the experiment.

6 · Rate how much this supports the alternative thoughts (from 0 to 100 per cent).

Introduction

Set agenda – *5 minutes*

Review homework – *5 to 10 minutes*

This week's task: Challenging dysfunctional assumptions – *30 minutes*

Review session – *5 to 10 minutes*

Set homework – *5 to 10 minutes*

Materials needed – Two or three copies of *Handouts 1 and 2 for Step 8*

Step 8 · Dysfunctional Assumptions

Introduction

This step is aimed at identifying dysfunctional assumptions, and then trying to help the client to overcome them. The nature of dysfunctional assumptions is described in Part 1 of this book. You need to familiarise yourself with this before the session. By this stage in therapy, you and the client will usually have begun to have some clear ideas of the areas in which the client's dysfunctional assumptions lie. When dealing with dysfunctional assumptions, it is important to help the client describe them in their own words. Dysfunctional assumptions follow common themes, but the ways individual clients describe and experience them are idiosyncratic. It is important to get the exact form of words from the client. So, in this step, it is important to use Socratic dialogue as this will help in ensuring that the client describes the dysfunctional assumptions accurately. As the challenging of dysfunctional assumptions is a slow and complicated process, taking several weeks, you will need to spend several sessions on this step. You should warn the client about the slow pace, so that they do not become too despondent.

Set agenda

Begin the session in the usual way, by agreeing the agenda for this week. This will again include the usual things – reviewing the homework; setting tasks for the week; review of the session, and setting the homework. Explain that this week's task will concern dysfunctional assumptions.

Review homework from last week

The homework from the previous week is likely to be the completion of a behavioural experiment, or challenging negative automatic thoughts. Check how this went, and discuss any difficulties the client may have had. If they had major difficulties, they may need some help. If the behavioural experiment or challenging the negative automatic thought was concerning a key issue, then you may need to spend this session dealing with that, rather than dealing with any underlying assumptions. However, behavioural experiments can be used to work on underlying assumptions, and it may be that much of the content of their negative automatic thoughts reflects underlying assumptions anyway. If this seems to be the case, then it would make sense to integrate the reformulation of the behavioural experiment with dealing with the underlying assumptions. Their negative automatic thoughts will have been generated by a dysfunctional assumption anyway, so now is the time to start to work on them.

This week's task

The main task for this session is to describe the nature of dysfunctional assumptions. Much of what you need to know is contained in Part 1 of this book.

Explain to the client that dysfunctional assumptions are not always as obvious as their automatic thoughts. They are often best described and recognised when they are stated in the format of 'If ... then ...' or 'should' statements. For example, a dysfunctional assumption that could be associated with depression might be, 'If I am not successful at everything I do, then everyone will dislike me.' As you can see, in this statement it is possible for the client to avoid the effects of the dysfunctional assumption. They can only do this by always being successful. Being successful is usually possible for most people, but always being successful is a very tall order. However, sometimes people manage to be successful for the majority of the time, and therefore avoid the consequence of the dysfunctional assumption for them – that is, in this example, of people disliking them. Because of this they remain free of depression for long periods, and it is only when they start to fail that the dysfunctional assumption starts to act. They start to think that people dislike them, and this makes them feel sad and depressed.

As you can see, dysfunctional assumptions tend to be extreme. A more balanced approach to thinking is less extreme, so the aim with the above assumption would be to allow the client some escape routes. A more balanced belief would be something like this: 'I should always try to succeed, but this may not always be possible. Although people may respect me for succeeding, it is not the only thing they judge me on.' This means that if they fail they would not automatically start to think that they will not be liked, and so the chance of them becoming depressed is less.

The purpose of dealing with dysfunctional assumptions is to prevent the susceptibility to depression in the future. It is the dysfunctional assumptions that generate the negative automatic thoughts that in turn lead to depression. Over the weeks that you have met with the client, you will hopefully have started to identify the common themes that occur in the client's thought records. Also, you will probably have already identified the areas in which the client's dysfunctional assumptions belong from the behavioural experiments. Over the next few sessions, you will help them to become more aware of these and start to tackle them.

It is often helpful to explain to the client that the dysfunctional assumptions frequently begin in early life. As a child begins to make sense of the world, they try to organise their experiences into familiar patterns. In the very early stages of life, the most formative experiences are visual. However, from the second or third year, as the child begins to develop language they start to categorise their experiences. They often develop unsophisticated rules that cover broad categories, such as touching hot things causes pain. Children also learn from people around them. Of course, this is usually their family.

The rules a child develops early in life may not reflect the world as it really is. For example, a child may believe that dogs bite. While this is sometimes true, dogs can also be very friendly and affectionate animals, and it is only with time that children can learn to discriminate between which dogs are friendly and which are not. As you can see, they have to develop a more complicated rule concerning dogs.

This elaboration of rules and beliefs carries on throughout life, but it is most prominent in the first 20 years. It is during this period of life, childhood and adolescence, that the client developed their rules for living. These are called assumptions, and when they are formulated in such a way that they become a problem to the client, we call them dysfunctional assumptions.

Dysfunctional assumptions can often be identified by using the downward arrow technique described in Figure 6 (Step 6). You can also help the client identify assumptions by asking them to review their thought records. In order for them to do this, you can use *Handout 1*. They are instructed to try to identify different negative automatic thoughts that are connected in some way. As negative automatic thoughts can be about themselves, others, or the world around them, the client should try to organise their negative automatic thoughts into these categories (as in the headings of *Handout 1*).

To help the client identify other assumptions, try to look for repetitive patterns of behaviour. For example, is there something that the client avoids doing? If this is the case, you may be able to construct an assumption with them by adding an 'if I [insert whatever they are not doing], then...'. The avoidance may be behavioural, a thought, or a feeling. Similarly, repetitive behaviours or rigid coping strategies might also indicate a dysfunctional assumption. For example, 'If I always agree with others then people will like me.' Here, the repetitive behaviour is the constant agreeing and lack of assertion. Another way of identifying dysfunctional assumptions is when two opposite behaviours or thoughts are linked — for example, 'If I shout at someone because I'm angry, then I should make up for it by doing something nice for them.' If the two negative automatic thoughts described above were part of the client's thinking, then on *Handout 1 of Step 8* the client might write:

I am only worthwhile if I do what other people want.
Others are more worthy or important than me.
The world is full of people who are better than me and more worthwhile.

In this example, the three areas are very connected. This is not always the case, but there should always be a link between the three areas in the client's mind, and you should try to understand this link with them. If, for example, the client says the world is a punitive place, you should try to identify why they believe this. It could be because they experience the need to please others as punishment. This may help you identify how they came to believe that they need to please others to be liked.

After you have identified a dysfunctional assumption with the client, you need to help them develop different beliefs. These new beliefs or assumptions should be more functional for the client. To do this you need to:

1 Have the client state the dysfunctional assumption clearly.

2 Encourage the client to make a list of possible alternative ways of being. Ask questions such as 'How would you like it to be?' and 'How would you like to be?'

3 Next, explore with the client the benefits of having the dysfunctional assumptions, and then the costs of the dysfunctional assumptions. There will always be both costs and benefits. When you are exploring the benefits, these may not be that apparent for the client. Remember that the dysfunctional assumptions are sometimes culturally approved of, and so benefits may be so obvious and common that the client may not recognise them.

4 Help the client to define realistic goals for themselves concerning their new beliefs. These should be defined very carefully, so that the client can clearly recognise what is required and when they have achieved a goal. You can get them to imagine what it would be like if they had this new belief. Encourage them to create a vivid image of this in their mind. They should describe what consequences the new belief has for their behaviour. For example, in the case above concerning the need to do things to please others, the client is asked what alternative ways of responding they can think of in the various situations they will come across. As their dysfunctional assumptions can operate in many areas of their life, you need to try to get them to describe how the new behaviour would change in different situations requiring different responses.

5 Help the client construct a behavioural experiment to test out their new beliefs once you have helped them develop a list of responses to situations. When they have performed the behavioural experiment, discuss it in the next session and identify what they learnt during the experiment. Did the experiment support or contradict their dysfunctional assumptions and their new beliefs? Identify any difficulties encountered, and develop solutions for these. Get them to build in reminders and reinforcements for their new ways of thinking. Encourage the client to think about what new principles are associated with their new beliefs.

6 Encourage them to set up more behavioural experiments to further test their beliefs. The client will need to conduct many behavioural experiments over time as their new beliefs are fragile at first, and need much practice for them to become strengthened and replace their dysfunctional assumptions.

7 Ensure the client records new evidence they identify from behavioural experiments and also from other sources (they may still be completing Daily Thought Records). They can do this on *Handout 2*.

As part of testing out their new beliefs, the client needs to be helped to accept ambiguity – that is, that in many situations the outcome is often uncertain and unknown, because other people are involved. The other person's responses cannot always be known. Therefore, the client can sometimes only infer what the response is, and needs to be able to tolerate doubt about situations. They will not always know what the other person thinks or feels. This can be an uncomfortable experience for the client, as in the past they may often have jumped to conclusions as a result of their dysfunctional assumptions. This left them without doubt about situations, even though their conclusions were often based on little or no evidence. You need to encourage the client to accept the discomfort associated with doubt.

Another way of working with dysfunctional assumptions is to construct a continuum of beliefs and behaviour. This is done in the following way:

1 Identify the dysfunctional assumptions.

2 Identify the alternative way of thinking, by asking such questions as 'How would you like to be?'; 'How would you like things to be?'; 'How would you like others to be?'; 'If you or others weren't this way, how would you or others be?'.

3 Draw a continuum for one alternative belief. You need to do this in a collaborative way. Effectively a continuum is drawn out on a piece of paper as a line with dysfunctional assumptions written at one end and new beliefs at the other.

4 Get the client to mark where they are on the continuum at present, and ask them to mark where they would like to be. Also ask them about other people they are close to – 'Where would they put them on the continuum?' Ask how they would have placed themselves in different situations and in different times.

5 Get the client to talk about the continuum. Ask them 'What can you make of this?', 'What does this tell you?'.

The process of challenging dysfunctional assumptions takes a long time, usually over several months. You should ensure that the client is aware of this, as otherwise the slow pace of progress may dishearten them. You need to make sure that they persevere over months, so that make the new beliefs become second nature.

Review the session

At the end of each session, check that the client has understood the content of the session and clarify anything that they have not understood. As the sessions progress, the client should find the challenging of their dysfunctional assumptions easier, and they should have less difficulty with the information gained in the session.

Set homework

The homework will flow naturally from the session. It could be collecting evidence about new beliefs, doing a behavioural experiment, or designing a behavioural experiment. At this stage there will always be plenty of material in the session to structure homework around. You need to adjust the amount and difficulty of the homework according to the client's progress. You aim to push the client as far as they can manage to maximise their improvement. This can be gauged by gradually increasing the homework until the client is not coping with all that you have set, or seems to be struggling with it. At this stage you take the level back a little to a manageable level.

As usual, the homework should be agreed with the client to ensure a collaborative approach.

Identifying Dysfunctional Assumptions

Using the Daily Thought Records that you have completed over the weeks, and identify themes that connect two or more thought records. Pay particular attention to negative automatic thoughts that occur frequently. Complete the sentences below in order to summarise the negative automatic thoughts.

1 I am _____

_____

_____

2 Others are _____

_____

_____

3 The world is _____

_____

_____

Speechmark **P**

Collecting the Evidence that Supports my New Belief

Write out your new belief (assumption), and then record any event that supports it, no matter how small or tentative this may be. Continue to do this over the coming weeks.

State new belief

_____

_____

Evidence that supports the new belief

1 _____

2 _____

3 _____

4 _____

5 _____

6 _____

7 _____

8 _____

9 _____

10 _____

11 _____

12 _____

Step 9 · Problem Solving

Introduction

People are constantly faced with problems to solve. Most of these do not pose too much difficulty. However, individuals are occasionally faced with more difficult problems for which they cannot easily find a solution. This step describes a tried and tested method for solving problems. This method can sometimes take quite a bit of time to go through, but it is a very effective.

Set agenda

Begin the session in the usual way by agreeing the agenda for this week. This will again include the usual things: reviewing the homework; tasks for this week; review of the session, and setting the homework.

Review homework from last week

By now the client should be working on various problems in their life using the techniques described earlier. Check that they are not having any problems and, if necessary, set aside time to deal with any difficulty that arises. They will usually have become reasonably competent at using the methods already described.

If you have had to introduce this step earlier because the client is having difficulty in solving a particular problem, ensure that they have completed the previous week's homework and only use this session if it is going to help the client move forward. This will only be because a serious problem is hampering their progress and preventing the client from moving forward.

This week's task

In this step, you teach the client how to solve problems using the method outlined below. This can be quite a slow way of doing things, but it is very effective, so the time is well spent. The client works through the following stages:

1 *Problem Definition.* Defining the problem may seem an obvious thing to do, but often people do not see the problem clearly. Ask the client various questions. When does it occur and for how long? Why does it happen – what brings it on or ends it? What happens, or what do other people do, or how do they respond? Where does it happen?

How does it happen? What is the sequence of events? What precipitates the problem? Who else is involved or is a major player? As they are answering these questions, get them to write down the answers, and then formulate the problem in a logical way. For example: 'My problem is that I cannot persuade my daughter [the who] to stop smoking [the what] in the house [where] when I am not at home [when].' You could use *Handout 2* for this.

2 *Brainstorming.* Now spend at least 10 minutes 'brainstorming' the problem. Brainstorming means thinking of as many solutions to a problem as possible. The solutions at this stage can be as bizarre and wild as you like. The more solutions generated, and the more varied they are, the better. So, for the example problem this may include solutions such as throwing the daughter out; searching her every time she comes in to ensure that she does not have any cigarettes on her, and then locking her in when you go out; or having a long discussion with her. Just because a solution appears extreme does not mean it should be excluded at this stage. Write down all the solutions. When at home, the client can get help with this task from family and friends.

3 *Rating the desirability of the solution.* Next the client rates each solution on a scale of 0 to 10. Ten would indicate a solution they feel is extremely desirable and practical. After this, select the top three or four solutions. These are the ones that the client now chooses from.

4 *Examining the practicality of a solution.* The client should now create two lists relating to each selected solution. The first will include all the forces that will help achieve the solution. Some of these may already be present or operating. The second list will include all those forces working against the solution.

   Using the example above, if the proposed solution was to talk to her daughter about her smoking, then the following analysis of forces could result. These lists should be as comprehensive as possible. Separate lists should be made for each proposed solution.

FORCES FOR	FORCES AGAINST
(a) I have a good relationship with her.	**(a)** Her boyfriend will try to sabotage.
(b) She likes to be part of making decisions.	**(b)** She is not often around when I am.
(c) My partner will support me.	

5 *Develop strategies for decreasing hindering forces and increasing helping forces.* The client then looks at ways of reducing any hindering forces and strengthening any that help bring about the solution. This can be done by using Socratic dialogue with the client.

6 *Choosing the best solution.* On completing this process for all the selected solutions, the client now chooses the best one and draws up a plan of action with a *definite* timetable. From the example above:

(a) Talk with partner tonight during evening meal.

(b) Talk to boyfriend tomorrow (in order to reduce the possibility of him sabotaging the solution).

(c) Discuss problem with daughter when we go out together on Wednesday.

Note that specific times and situations are chosen, along with specific actions. It is important to ensure that the client is clear about what they are going to do and whether they have completed the task correctly.

7 *Review the outcome of the solution.* Did it work? If not, why not? Could the solution be improved? Have the actions generated any new ideas? If the solution is ineffective, choose another solution from the shortlist and implement that.

Review the session

Ask the client to tell you what they have learnt about problem-solving. Clarify any points as necessary. Check how they felt about this session and their progress. Ensure that they understand the homework and feel confident to attempt it.

Set homework

From the session today you will probably have generated a problem to be solved and decided on a course of action. The implementation of the solution will therefore form the homework. If you did not have time to complete the problem-solving task, then the completion of the problem-solving process would also form part of the homework.

Problem-Solving

1 Define the problem in as clear a way as possible. Ask yourself, Who? What? Why? Where? When?

2 Brainstorming – think of as many solutions as possible, the more the better. Also make them as varied as you can. At this stage, it does not matter if the solutions are practical.

3 Rate each solution according to its desirability.

4 Assess the practicality of each solution. Write down a list of factors both for and against each solution. See if there are any ways of the overcoming the factors that hinder a particular solution.

5 Choose the best solution. Develop a plan of action. Implement the plan.

6 Review the outcome. If it was effective, then the problem is solved. If it wasn't, look at where it went wrong and try to develop a plan to overcome this. If the action plan produced new information, then it may be necessary to go through the whole process again.

Record Sheet For Problem-Solving

Problem Definition:

	Possible solutions	Factors for	Factors against
1			
2			
3			
4			
5			
6			
7			
8			
9			
10			

Choose ideal solution and develop an action plan.

Did the solution work? What do you need to change? What did I learn?

Devise new plan?

Step 10 · Preparing for the Future

Introduction

Set agenda – *5 minutes*

Review homework – *5 to 10 minutes*

This week's task: Describing the development of relapse plans – *30 minutes*

Review session – *5 to 10 minutes*

Set homework – *5 to 10 minutes*

Materials needed – Two copies of *Handout 1 for Step 10*

Introduction

You have now taught the client all they need to know to overcome their depression. They should have improved significantly, but will probably still have some depressive symptoms. They should know when they are experiencing negative automatic thoughts, and also be aware of their dysfunctional assumptions. They will have challenged their own dysfunctional assumptions and be reasonably confident in using the skills you have both worked on over the previous weeks. However, the client will need to keep up their efforts over the coming months, and this step will help them develop an action plan. The aim of the action plan will be to help the client to:

1 Recognise any early signs of the depression reoccurring.
2 Identify times in the future when they may be at risk of depression.
3 Continue to strengthen their new beliefs.

During this step it is wise to reduce the frequency of sessions to alternate weeks, and then to every four weeks. This allows the client to get used to the idea of the therapy ending.

Set agenda

Begin the session in the usual way by agreeing the agenda for this week. This will again include the usual things: reviewing the homework, tasks for the week, a review of the session and setting the homework. Explain that today's task will be concerned with planning for the future, and developing an action plan to deal with potential relapses.

Review homework from last week

By this stage the client will have been working on the various aspects of their dysfunctional assumptions. They may have been challenging their dysfunctional assumptions directly, or using behavioural experiments. They should discuss how these have been going with you, as they will have been working on them as homework between sessions. By the time you have taken the decision to move on to Step 10, they should have been managing their homework reasonably well. Therefore, you are unlikely to encounter many problems at this stage.

This week's task

Start this week's task by reviewing the progress the client has made. Identify with the client the new skills and beliefs they have developed. Explain that they now have all the skills and knowledge they need to defeat their depression. Then tell them it is time to prepare for the future, so that depression need never take over their life again. They will almost certainly have times when things do not go well for them, but this is natural. However, rather than sinking into a depressive state they will now be able to deal with matters as they arise. To be able to do this they will have to consciously make an effort to use the skills they have learnt; be aware of the situations that have made them depressed in the past, and develop a plan of action. The aim of this step is to help them do this.

Ask the client to review their profile of depression, which they completed in Step 1. Go through this with the client, and try to identify the sequence of the onset of symptoms. Birchwood *et al*, 2000, have developed the concept of a relapse signature. They postulate that any individual who has recurrent episodes of psychosis has a characteristic pattern of onset to each episode. There may be prodromal symptoms that are usually non-specific (Smith *et al* 1992; Lam & Wong 1997). For example, wearing different clothes; different tastes in food or music; sleep problems; decreased energy. Any of these symptoms could occur at any time, and do not in themselves indicate that relapse is likely. However, if four or five of them occur together, then the chances of relapse are high.

Try to identify with the client the very early changes they experienced when they became depressed. If they had experienced depression before this episode, see if there were similar symptoms then. As you discuss these ideas, you may be able to start to develop a relapse signature, or at least identify some changes that occur at a stage early in the client's depression. The client should write these down on *Handout 1*.

Next, develop an action plan with the client to deal with signs of imminent relapse and times of risk. This, in effect, is what Birchwood *et al* would call the relapse drill. This will mean identifying ways of preparing for stressful times and dealing with early signs of depression. Help the client think through the things they can do. This may involve looking back at the activity schedules they have competed during their course of treatment, and selecting things from them that have helped. They should identify negative automatic thoughts and dysfunctional assumptions that they would expect to occur in these circumstances. You and the client should prepare cards with their negative automatic thoughts and dysfunctional assumptions written on them, and the way that they can challenge these cognitively. These would be a personalised version of *Handout 1 for Step 6*.

You and the client should review environmental factors, and see whether anything can be done about these. For example, they could reduce stress by taking a holiday, or they could cut down the amount of their work. Their family and friends are often of great help. However, they can also be a source of stress, and identifying how they can help or how they hinder is necessary. Through discussion with the client, you should be able to develop ways of making use of their support and removing any hindrances. These should be written into their action plans.

In case these measures fail, the client needs to have a fall-back plan. This may be the introduction of the full cognitive therapy programme you have just completed with them. As they may well have all of their handouts, they may be able to do this alone. But they may need a few booster sessions, and it may be possible for you to offer them the opportunity to contact you to arrange these without the need for referral. They may also need to see their doctor to explore whether they need medication or have a change in medication.

The important thing is that the client understands the need to act early in the course of the illness, as this will mean less suffering and easier treatment. The signs and symptoms that make up the relapse signature may be non-specific, and therefore the client may not become depressed. Thus any action at a very early stage should be less intrusive, and be initiatives that are generally helpful. For example, ensuring they eat and sleep properly, do not overwork, and so on. More time-consuming and disruptive measures like keeping full thought records should be kept for later.

The action plan should be devised with the principle of early preventative measures in mind. The actions need to be placed in order and, where possible, have a time frame associated with them. A plan might be:

1 Ensure I have sufficient rest by always taking a 45-minute lunch break away from my desk at work, and by being in bed by 22.30.
2 If this does not work within one week, use the flash cards about my negative automatic thought and dysfunctional assumptions each day for the next two weeks.
3 If no better, reduce the amount of time at work or take a holiday, and start to fully implement the cognitive therapy programme.

After the action plan is formulated, and as the interval between the last sessions grows, the client may have the opportunity to test their plan if they experience dips in their mood. This can be a very valuable learning experience for the client. They often feel much more confident in implementing the relapse plan when they know they can discuss it with you if it does not work as they would like.

Review the session

Ask the client about their views concerning the plan to end therapy. Ensure that this has not caused them too much distress. Ask them to summarise what you have covered in the session, and identify any difficulties they may have experienced.

Set homework

The homework will follow on from the session's content. Where you have got to in the session will determine the exact form of the homework. The client may need to continue to develop their relapse signature, or possibly work on their relapse plan. In later sessions in this step it may be that they will be using the plan as part of their homework. You and the client will need to decide together what is appropriate for homework.

Action Plan

List of early signs	Actions to deal with symptoms
1	1
2	2
3	3
4	4
5	5
6	6
7	7
8	8
9	9
10	10
List situations that pose a risk of depression	Actions to deal with risk
1	1
2	2
3	3
4	4
5	5
6	6
7	7
8	8
9	9
10	10

Additional Information

Part 3

Drug Treatment and Approaches to Medication Adherence

Drug treatment

As mentioned earlier in this book, biological factors may play a major part in the onset of depression. Even when there are obvious stressful events causing the depression, it may be advisable for the client to seek their doctor's advice concerning medication. In the main, drugs and the advice given in this book are complementary – they help each other. Therefore, any medications that the client may be taking should not interfere with their treatment regime with you. You should encourage the client to follow the instructions their doctor has given them regarding their medication. Most anti-depressants do not work immediately and the client will have to be on them for up to three weeks before they notice improvement. Also, the client will need to keep taking medication for a few months after getting better. There are many anti-depressant drugs available, and below you will find information about many of the more commonly prescribed ones. Anti-depressants, like all other drugs, have a scientific name and one or more brand names. The brand name will appear in parentheses below.

This information is provided to enable you to discuss any concerns the client may have or mention. The information is not comprehensive, and the client should always be advised to discuss any major concerns with their doctor. Their pharmacist may also be able to give them advice about their medication. Most medication now comes with a leaflet describing the medication, side effects, usual dose range and instructions for taking it. However, the client may be concerned about some symptom that may represent a side effect of the medication, and if you are aware of whether it is a side effect or not, you may be able to advise the client as to whether they need to see their GP for further advice. More information can be found in the British National Formulary (2003).

Tricyclic anti-depressants (TCA)
Until a few years ago, these were the main anti-depressants in use. They are very effective. There are several anti-depressants in this group:

Amitriptyline	(Tryptizol)
Imipramine	(Tofranil)
Clomipramine	(Anafranil)
Doxepin	(Sinequan)
Dothiepin	(Dothapax, Prothiaden)

| Lofepramine | (Gamanil) |
| Trimipramine | (Surmontil) |

Most of these drugs remain in the bloodstream long enough to make it possible to take them only once a day – although the client will usually need more than one tablet. Most of them can cause side effects. The side effects are usually mild and more of a nuisance than a serious concern. However, they can occasionally be more troublesome. The main side effects are:

1 *Constipation* – If this becomes a major problem the client can be advised to try to increase the fibre content in their diet. Suggest eating wholemeal bread, cereals (Weetabix, Shredded Wheat, Shreddies, Allbran, Branflakes, and so on), brown rice, wholemeal pasta, and more fruit and vegetables. If this is ineffective, they should seek the advice of their doctor.

2 *Dry mouth* – The client can try sucking sweets, chewing gum, or taking regular sips of water. This side effect usually gets less after a few days.

3 *Blurred vision* – The client may find it difficult to focus on reading and watching the television. This tends to be intermittent and usually improves after a few days. No harm is done to their eyes, so they do not need to worry about this.

4 *Sedation* – As many of these drugs are sedative, the client may be advised to take their medication at bedtime, especially if the depression has affected their sleep. This could therefore be a help rather than a hindrance. Some anti-depressants are less likely to cause sedation, so if it is a major problem the client should be encouraged to talk to their doctor, who may be able to recommend a different anti-depressant.

5 *Weight gain* – Dieting does not often help if the client is eating normally. They may just have to put up with the weight gain until it is time to stop their medication. A change in medication can be considered, but unfortunately this is a problem with many anti-depressants. If the anti-depressants are clearly of benefit, then you should encourage the client to continue with them. Give them support with a sensible diet plan, or advice, or inform them where they can get the appropriate advice.

6 *Low blood pressure* – This is unusual in younger people. It tends to occur when the client gets up from sitting or lying down, and their blood pressure drops, making them feel faint. Getting up more slowly, and steadying themselves, helps. The blood pressure usually comes up again within a few seconds and then things will be normal again. If this is a serious problem, the client needs to see their doctor as soon as possible, for further advice.

7 *Difficulty in passing urine* – This usually only occurs in older men, and then only rarely. If this becomes a problem the client needs to see their doctor.

8 *Sweating*.

All of these side effects tend to subside with time, and become less troublesome if the dose is built up over a few days.

SSRIs

SSRIs stands for Specific Serotonin Reuptake Inhibitors, which describes their action in the brain. Their action is more precise than the TCAs', and this results in less side effects. These drugs are the ones most prescribed. They are taken once a day, usually in the morning or at lunchtime with food. Drugs in this group include:

Citalopram	(Cipramil)
Fluoxetine	(Prozac)
Fluvoxamine	(Faverin)
Paroxetine	(Seroxat)
Sertraline	(Lustral)

They are equally effective and the only common side effect is nausea. This affects 10 to 20 per cent of people. Nausea may be less of a problem if the drugs are taken with food. Occasionally, the drugs may disturb the client's sleep, in which case taking them earlier in the day will help. Sometimes the client may experience a discontinuation syndrome if they stop these medications abruptly. This syndrome includes headache, nausea, paraesthesia, dizziness and anxiety.

MAOI

MAOI stands for Mono Amine Oxidase Inhibitor. Again, this describes the action of the drug. MAOIs are less popular than other anti-depressants. Since their action is different from other anti-depressants, they may be tried when others have failed. They are also said to be useful in atypical depressions, in which anxiety may be a central feature.

The side effect profile is similar to that of the TCAs (see above). However, they also have another complication, which is why they are used less commonly. MAOIs interact with a substance called tyramine. This is present in certain foods, which means that these foods have to be avoided. Foods on this list include cheese, yeast products (including Marmite, Bovril, Oxo), gravy, pickled herrings and certain red wines, especially chianti. These drugs also interact with codeine and similar drugs which are often found in painkillers and cough and cold cures. The client needs to check with the chemist when buying such medicines that they are safe to take with MAOIs. The drugs in this group include:

Isocarboxazid	
Moclobamide	(Manerix)
Phenelzine	(Nardil)
Tranylcypromine	(Parnate)

Moclobamide is a newer type of MAOI, which has a decreased interaction with tyramine, therefore allowing small quantities of these foods to be eaten.

Others

There are other anti-depressants that do not fall into the groups above. They include:

Trazodone	(Molipaxin)
Venlafaxine	(Efexor)
Reboxetine	(Edronax)
Mirtazapine	(Zispin)
Nefazedone	(Dutonin)

These drugs are not related to each other, and can have different side effects. However, they are all newer than the older anti-depressants such as TCAs and MAOIs, and tend to be less likely to cause side effects. For further information on these drugs, the client or therapist can access the website of the British National Formulary at www.bnf.org.uk, or discuss the drug with their GP or pharmacist.

Mood stabilisers

These drugs are mainly used with people who have recurrent depressions. They are not usually prescribed by GPs. The aim is to prevent rather than cure depression. However, they may be combined with other anti-depressants if the depression does not respond to a single drug. If they are being used to prevent depression, then they will need to be taken for months or years. The five drugs used are:

Lithium	(Priadel, Camcolil, Phasal, Liskonium and Litarex)
Carbamazepine	(Tegretol)
Valproate	(Epilim)
Gabatentin	
Lamotragine	

The last four are also used for epilepsy. This does not mean that the client's depression is in any way related to epilepsy; it is just that these drugs also have a beneficial effect in recurrent mood disorders.

Lithium is an unusual drug, because it is a simple element and therefore not metabolised by the body. The only way the body gets rid of lithium is by excretion in the urine. Lithium is also very toxic in overdose, so its level in the blood is routinely monitored by blood tests. It has many side effects, even though many people can take it without any untoward symptoms. The client should discuss any concerns with their doctor, as the monitoring of this drug needs extra care.

All of these drugs are used mainly for the treatment of recurrent depression, so the client will be on them long term. Long-term medication has implications for compliance, and these are discussed next.

Approaches to Medication Adherence

The therapist will not be responsible for prescribing the client's medication, but can help the client to adhere to their doctor's recommendations. Adherence is most likely to occur if there is an agreement between the client's ideas about their illness and their doctor's instructions. Therefore, the therapist needs to establish whether the client's perspective of the prescribed treatment is that it is acceptable, understandable and manageable. The client's beliefs about their illness, and their appraisal of their need to take medication will need to be reassessed at regular intervals. Continued adherence to medication is only likely to occur when the client's beliefs about their illness coincide with their doctor's advice.

In the health beliefs model of Becker & Maimon (1975), there are four main beliefs contributing to the likelihood of an individual adhering to their prescribed medication (see Table 13).

TABLE 13 · FACTORS AFFECTING MEDICATION ADHERENCE

1 · Perceived benefits of adherence (for instance, possibility of being kept symptom-free).

2 · Perceived barriers to adherence (for instance, stigma or problems with side effects).

3 · Perceived susceptibility to illness (for instance, a belief that they are likely to experience a relapse).

4 · Perceived severity of the outcome (for instance, a belief that the relapse would have negative consequences).

Individuals are more likely to continue with their medication if the perceived threat of the illness is high, and the perceived benefits of treatment exceed the perceived barriers. The client's beliefs associated with adherence may be specific to illness or treatment (for example, 'Doctors do more harm than good'), but many of the views that influence a client's adherence are representative of their general rules or assumptions (for example, 'I must be in control; I must do everything perfectly').

A client's belief will be influenced by any number of modifying factors. Some are described in Table 14.

TABLE 14 · FACTORS AFFECTING THE CLIENT'S BELIEFS ASSOCIATED WITH TAKING MEDICATION
1 · Personality attributes
2 · Influence of significant others
3 · Cultural beliefs and context
4 · General health motivations
5 · General orientation towards medicine.

The model also states that individuals need a prompt to engage in health-related behaviours. These prompts may be internal – such as a recognition of prodromal symptoms – or they may be external, such as statements made by others, or media references to illness or medication.

Assessment of health beliefs

You should discuss with the client their views about their illness, and any fears about treatment. You need to assess how they perceive the threat of the illness. This includes the client's view of their susceptibility to the illness and its severity. You need to assess the benefits the client perceives the treatment will have, and also any barriers to accepting treatment. Any modifying factors should be identified, and also any cues that may prompt the individual to take their medication. You need to retain an open mind and not to assume that you will know the answers to any of these questions.

Interventions to enhance adherence

The role of ensuring compliance with medication is essentially that of the client's doctor. However, you may be seeing the client more frequently than their doctor, and the client may in fact talk to you more about their medication. In Tables 15 and 16 are some behavioural and cognitive methods for increasing compliance.

TABLE 15 · BEHAVIOURAL STRATEGIES FOR INCREASING MEDICATION ADHERENCE

1 · Simplify the regime. The easier it is for the client to take their medication, the more likely they are to take it.

2 · Behavioural prompt. This might be a note stuck in a prominent place that is visited daily, such as the bathroom mirror, or the linking of taking medication with a routine daily activity.

3 · Rehearsal strategies. In this, the client visualises each step in their medication routine, and by doing so may expose barriers to adherence. You and the client can then plan ahead and rehearse coping strategies.

4 · Monitoring and diary-keeping. The client monitors their taking of medication by keeping a simple diary of what they have taken and when.

TABLE 16 · COGNITIVE STRATEGIES FOR INCREASING MEDICATION ADHERENCE

1 · Homework assignments to ascertain the client's experience of medication and any barriers to medication. These could take the form of asking the client to fill in a record of their medication-taking, along with any thoughts, side effects and other effects (whether beneficial or not) associated with their medication.

2 · Identifying any negative automatic thoughts associated with medication, and dealing with them in the ways described earlier. Common themes associated with non-compliance are autonomy and control.

3 · Developing an action plan to deal with situations when the client is likely to be non-compliant with medication.

You should be as flexible as possible, and encourage the client to talk to their doctor about any concerns that they may have regarding their medication. If you think it would be helpful, you can offer to talk about the client's medication with their doctor. Another way of handling this is to rehearse what the client will discuss with their doctor, so that any anxiety that they will not be listened to can be reduced.

Scott and Wright (1997) and Scott (1999) advocate developing a cost benefit analysis of taking medication. In this, the client and therapist draw up a table that covers the advantages and disadvantages of taking medication, and the advantages and disadvantages of not taking medication. The therapist has to draw the client's attention to the advantages of taking medication and the disadvantages of not taking medication. It is sometimes necessary to seek a third party opinion from someone the client trusts, to help them appreciate the advantages of taking medication.

Management of Suicide

'Suicide is the intentional act of taking one's own life, either as a result of mental illness or of various motivations which outweigh the instinct to continue to live.'

The facts in Table 17 are vital for anyone involved in the management of suicide. The treatment of a person at risk of suicide depends upon accurate diagnosis and establishing, by a full clinical assessment, the underlying causes. Also necessary are a thorough family and social history, and evaluation of mental state. A physical investigation is also important, as factors such as inadequate diet and increased substance abuse are linked to the likelihood of suicide.

Suicide is an emotive subject, and being faced with someone who is intent on taking their life can evoke a variety of personal and professional issues. A professional approach employs a positive focus without value judgements or opinions. A positive attitude towards the prevention of suicide is paramount. When a suicidal person talks to a therapist it is likely that they have had suicidal thoughts for a significant period and can be ambivalent about the process of dying. It is vital to restore hope, even though their problems may appear to be insurmountable. A person at risk should seek the advice of a professional regarding suicide and their thoughts.

Assessment and risk factors

The risk factors are common, and therefore prediction of which individual will commit suicide is complicated. Risk factors must be acknowledged, although they do not necessarily indicate the causes of suicide. For example, a person's symptoms could be present in all of the risk areas, but not be as intense as those of a person who falls into just one of the risk categories. These risk factors are used as a guideline, and are most effective in predicting the risk of suicide in the long term.

When assessing an individual and their risk of suicide, it is helpful for the therapist to imagine the feelings that someone has when their only option is to end their life. The despair and unhappiness that we may experience infrequently as a result of significant disturbances in our lives are a constant factor in the life of a suicidal person. In hoping to understand and assess the severity of suicidal symptoms and behaviour, the therapist must be open to these intense negative emotions. People who are intent on killing themselves appear almost

TABLE 17 · FACTS ABOUT SUICIDE

1 · Suicide accounts for 1 per cent of all deaths in Britain (Williams & Morgan 1996).

2 · In general, the risk of suicide increases with age. This increase tends to be more gradual with women. Over the last 30 years, the suicide rate of men aged between 18 and 28 years has doubled (Williams & Morgan 1996).

3 · Suicide is the second most common cause of death in young males aged (15 to 34 years) (Williams & Morgan 1996).

4 · In Britain, the rate of suicide is highest between April and June (Williams & Morgan 1996).

5 · Men are three times as likely to kill themselves as women (Department of Health 1999).

6 · The commonest methods of suicide are hanging (men) and self-poisoning by overdose (women) (Department of Health 1999).

7 · The commonest drugs used in overdose in women were those prescribed to treat mental disorder (Department of Health 1999).

8 · The commonest diagnoses were depression, schizophrenia, personality disorder, and alcohol/drug dependency (Department of Health 1999).

9 · Twenty-four per cent of suicides had been in contact with mental health services in the week before death. At final contact, immediate risk of suicide was estimated to be low or absent in 85 per cent of cases of women (Department of Health 1999).

10 · Suicide is more common in people who live alone, and who are single, divorced or widowed women (Department of Health 1999).

11 · History of mental illness is one of the most important risk factors. Studies have identified depression as the most common mental disorder, and it has been shown that most people who have committed suicide have suffered from some form of psychiatric disorder before death.

resigned to death, having neglected all other options. The therapist's reaction to that person is vital, as it may be the final opinion that they seek.

There are basic features of psychiatric approaches that are effective in reducing the risk of suicide.

1 Thorough and accurate assessment, and prompt treatment of the illness, and appropriate aftercare.

2 In-patient admission is necessary for people who are at immediate risk of suicide.

3 Intensive nursing observations are usually implemented and, while this provides a safe environment for the person, it inhibits the establishing of relationships with staff. In order for relationships to be effective, the client and the therapist must be aiming for the same goal, with trust as a vital component in developing their rapport.

During assessment, it is important to register not only what the client is telling you, but also what they are not telling you. Poverty of emotional responsiveness, where there is a severe diminishment of emotional feelings, may be present. Apathy is frequently experienced, together with ambivalence to their environment and what is occurring. What the client is telling you may be incongruous with their behaviour and presentation. It is important to observe discrepancies between what is being said and the way the client behaves.

The stereotypical presentation of a suicidal person is someone who is experiencing a sense of hopelessness in themselves and the world around them, both holding little value or purpose. The client may not disclose ideas of suicide. The reluctance to disclose these thoughts may be to prevent any form of help that would take them away from the task they have set themselves – the task of dying. It may therefore be necessary for the therapist to judge the level of probable risk from comparing what the client says with their behaviour.

There is reluctance on the part of a majority of health professionals to discuss suicide. This is partly because, as a society, we find it an unacceptable practice, and on a more individual basis it leaves us with a sense of helplessness. In order to reduce the risk of suicide, the therapist needs to acknowledge the wish to die as a thought that is based on emotional responses to certain situations. As previous chapters in this book have illustrated, these thoughts can be changed into positive ways of thinking.

The important purpose of assessment is to gain an accurate and detailed picture of the client, and to create a trusting, empathic relationship, so they feel encouraged to disclose all to you.

The second stereotypical presentation appears in the form of self-harm. This manifests from the person's discontent with themselves, others, and the world in which they live. They may not necessarily experience the total despair and the commitment to suicide of the first group, but the level of risk is similarly severe. Deliberate self-harm, which is discussed in more detail later in this book, creates extreme reactions that may inhibit its effective management or treatment. There may be a long history of personality difficulties with frequent episodes of deliberate self-harm that have not been life-endangering. This group of people may not have a diagnosis of mental illness, but they experience difficulty in coping with stressful events or emotional disturbances. Their mood state becomes volatile, and their deliberate self-harm escalates. They are erroneously diagnosed as attention-seekers, becoming unpopular with health professionals and tending to become alienated. This is due to the dilemmas that they evoke in staff about how best to help them.

The guidelines in Table 18 may assist in ensuring an accurate and thorough assessment of a client.

When the initial assessment has been completed, the formulation of a plan of management is required. Ideally this will involve the therapist, the client, and other relevant parties (such as other health professionals and relatives). The plan should be realistic for the client. To formulate a care plan that is unachievable will increase the client's belief that they are a failure. Techniques used in resolving suicidal thinking include enabling the client to feel listened to in their own time; to feel accepted, despite what they may be disclosing to the therapist, and a sense of optimism.

Edwin Schneidman (1993) describes what is involved as 'Doing anything and everything possible to cater to the infantile idiosyncrasies, the dependency needs, the sense of pressure and futility, the feeling of hopelessness and helplessness that the individual is experiencing. In order to help the highly lethal person one should involve others and create activity around the person. Try to do what he or she wants done – and if that cannot be accomplished at least move in the direction of the desired goals to some substitute goals, that approximate to those which have been lost.'

It is imperative that a clear and concise presentation of the client is obtained. It is vital to understand what they perceive as problems, and the difficulties they may experience in addressing these problems. The therapist must acknowledge the client's point of view and their vulnerabilities.

Management of suicide in the community

Managing a suicidal client effectively in the community is based on a mutual acceptance of clear channels for communication, mutual support and trust. Information must be shared, and the relationship with the client must be supportive. There are advantages for the client in remaining in their home environment, as it encourages them, with support, to develop skills that will allow them to deal with issues that make their home life stressful. To remove a client

TABLE 18 · ASSESSMENT OF SUICIDE

1 · Ask them why they have decided to disclose now.

2 · Gradually discuss their reason for suicide.

3 · Ask the client what it is they want from you.

4 · Clarify what their intention is. Do they want to self-harm to relieve tension, or do they want to die?

5 · Ascertain if they have a plan and a method. Have they planned for the after-effects, such as funeral arrangements, or who will find them?

6 · How persistent is the thought of suicide?

7 · Do they have access to methods of killing themselves?

8 · Have they made an attempt on their lives previously?

9 · Gain information about their family and social history. Has there been suicide in their family? How much support do they have from family and friends?

10 · With their agreement, speak to friends and relatives to gain as much information as possible, so the client can identify the therapist as part of their supportive network.

11 · The therapist must be wary of negative or cynical attitudes, especially if the client has a long history of difficulties or non-compliance with treatment.

12 · Listen to what the client is saying. There is a tendency to want to reassure the client who may be experiencing a high level of distress. Reassurance may be interpreted as not acknowledging the severity of the distress that the client is suffering.

from a stressful and distressing home environment may be of benefit initially; however, it may encourage dependence on hospitals and healthcare professionals. Remaining at home is also less of a stigma than being admitted to the local psychiatric unit. This enables the client to retain as much of their 'normal' life as possible, and allows them to remain in close contact with their family.

Community management is not appropriate when the risk of suicide escalates to a critical level. Relatives will need the support and clinical knowledge of professionals. Staff are objective in the care of a suicidal patient and will implement their treatment based on sound clinical assessment, as opposed to emotional reasoning. If the client is intent on taking their own life, they may lie to their family about their whereabouts, or their compliance with medication. The family wanting them to recover may go along with this, as it reassures them. Families may find the stress of caring for a suicidal member overwhelming, and this may increase the stress for the client. It is of benefit for the client to be able to remove themselves from this situation, until the crisis level has significantly reduced. Wherever possible, the choice of where care is provided should be the client's preference, and where the most appropriate care for the individual is available.

The therapist should have adequate time to spend with the client, and should liaise with other professionals, who will need to be aware if the therapist is unable to meet with the client. Regular review of adherence and response to medication is important in the recovery period. Daily medication administration by a mental health professional may be considered in the initial stages.

An assessment of impulsive behaviour should be undertaken. People with a history of acts of deliberate self-harm, excessive alcohol or drug use, or from a severely volatile home environment, may indicate a need for a higher level of monitoring from professionals. Other indicators for close monitoring will include:

- Poor or dysfunctional family support
- Previous history of severe deliberate self-harm or suicide attempt
- Poor physical condition
- Significant recent events, such as the death of a loved one
- Fluctuation of degree of distress – difficult to predict risk.

The therapist may find a home visit of great advantage, as they will be able to experience another dimension of the client's life and build up a picture of the stresses they experience. It is also an opportunity to assess risks identified with the home environment. Is the client storing pills? Do they have access to weapons? Do they live in high-rise accommodation, or in a disturbed neighbourhood? Is there evidence of excessive alcohol or drug use?

Management of suicide in an in-patient setting

When all the risks have been assessed, it may indicate that the risk of suicide is too great to continue to support a client in the community, and that hospital admission is the safest option. The admission of a suicidal client to hospital requires thorough and accurate clinical assessment, which should be effectively documented. The level of observations should be determined, based on severity of risk, previous attempts, and how determined the client is. In developing a relationship with the client, if the risk is judged to be significant, the therapist needs to be honest as to why regular observations must be maintained. The client will respond to the feeling of being 'safe'. A treatment plan and appropriate observations need to be jointly agreed by the medical, nursing and other relevant staff. The treatment plan must have input from the client, and preferably from relatives. This encourages a sense of control, which promotes effort from the client. The ward to which the client is admitted will require a level of safety. This will include monitored exits, and quiet places for the client to be supervised intensely but without the feeling of being overpowered. The staff should exhibit a high level of professionalism, which will require a high level of morale and optimism. The staff should display non-judgemental empathy towards the client and their family. Effective teamwork among all disciplines is of paramount importance, particularly when working with clients who exhibit difficult behaviour. Clients are able to sense imbalance and disharmony within a team, and may respond in a negative way. The client should be presented with clear boundaries and structures so they can access support.

Suicide prevention

Stengel (1958) said 'suicidal behaviour represents a bid to communicate distress to key figures in an intimate social group.' An implication of this view is that where other groups would use less pathological forms of communication, the suicidal client is not able to do so. Suicide is a major cause of preventable death in Britain. If care professionals are aware of clients who are at risk, and are aware of how to assess and manage these risks, they stand a good chance of reducing the suicides that occur. Following a suicide, an investigation often reveals many of the signs that indicated it would occur. The ability to recognise this, and to put in place structures to prevent it, is where professionals need to focus.

The prediction of suicide is problematic however. There is a process of development that involves predisposing factors; perpetuating conditions; precipitating conditions, and preventative measures.

Healthcare professionals offer clients access to effective treatment. However, there are some clients who do not wish to utilise this facility, and therefore there should be options that allow clients other ways to obtain the help they need. One approach is to offer self-help materials. According to Cuijpers (1997), in self-help 'the patient receives a standardised treatment method with which he can help himself without major help from the therapist.' With this approach it is necessary that treatment be described in sufficient detail, so that the client can work it through independently. Books in which only information about depression is given cannot be used.

Self-help can be an effective method of delivering treatment. This can be supported by a therapist, but is effective in isolation. It can be used without the delay of referrals or waiting lists. An advantage of self-help is that the client can direct the speed at which they choose to progress. A session with a therapist, which is timed, can put pressure on the client to maximise that time. However, the self-help can be put down; the client can make a cup of tea and pick it up again. It also limits the stigma of seeking psychiatric referral, and promotes their privacy. This too will allow for the client to have a sense of control over their illness.

Disadvantages can also be present when using self-help. They will require a level of self-motivation that is not always present in a depressed client. It is important to access the most appropriate selection of self-help. A client with poor concentration or memory impairment may find a heavy book, full of statistics, difficult to work with, and give up. This in turn will increase their level of hopelessness. The advertising of such a book promotes a high level of hope that when you finish reading all your problems will be solved. This may create unrealistic expectations and lead to deterioration in the client. Examples of self-help books are listed at the end of this book.

Management of Self-harm

Self-harm involves the individual causing deliberate harm to their body. It can also be referred to as self-injury, self-mutilation, self-poisoning or para-suicide.

Presentations to casualty departments following episodes of self-harm are currently 150,000 annually, and this number is rising steadily. A high ratio of these clients suffer from a psychiatric disorder, and are 100 times more likely than the average member of the public to commit suicide in the year following their presentation (Hawton & Fagg 1988).

Deliberate self-harm is commonly perceived as a maladaptive behaviour – a strategy for coping with feelings of intolerable distress. It is also a method of communication for the client who is unable to express or manage their feelings. Self-harm is found in various groups of clients with differing diagnoses. Therapeutic relationships between the client and the therapist may prove difficult at times. This may be due to the therapist's inability to empathise and understand why people choose to cut their body, or to burn themselves. This can leave the professional with a profound sense of helplessness, and can result in a negative and pessimistic response to the client.

In order to make a difference, professionals must understand why some people have the need to self-harm. Table 19 lists reasons that people may self-harm.

Unfortunately, the response from professionals can be negative and punitive, thus leaving the client with higher levels of guilt, and feelings of low self-worth. It is important for the professional to respond in an objective and empathetic manner.

TABLE 19 · REASONS THAT PEOPLE SELF-HARM

1 · Control over some aspect of their life.

2 · Punishment.

3 · The sense of pain reassures them that they can experience an emotion, even of a negative nature.

4 · It acts as a physical focus point for emotional pain.

5 · A way of releasing anger. It is sometimes done for the purpose of getting help, or a particular reaction (Favazza & Conterio 1989).

For the therapist to be of use, they have to form an alliance with the client. A full psychosocial assessment of the client should be undertaken.

Self-harmers can be categorised into four groups:

1   Serious suicide risk – these are people who have a significant intent to kill themselves. This group can include profoundly depressed clients, or those who have a significant psychiatric disorder.

2   Self-mutilators – these are usually sufferers of a psychotic disorder, who may be responding to hallucinatory commands, or people who have an intense desire to mutilate a certain area of their body (usually genitalia or breasts).

3   Superficial self-harmers – these clients usually have extreme emotional issues, and have developed a maladaptive method of coping with them. Clients in this group will invariably have issues such as previous sexual abuse, low self-esteem, distorted self-image.

4   The final group of people who self-harm appear to be socially acceptable within our society. Their forms of self-harm, such as smoking, drinking and use of illicit drugs, can damage a person physically and emotionally. Such forms of self-harm affect a high proportion of society.

Assessment

People who self-harm will do so for many different reasons. There are various risk factors to consider when working with the client, which are listed in Table 20.

TABLE 20 · FACTORS AFFECTING SELF-HARM
1 · Underlying psychiatric condition
2 · Poor social support
3 · Previous or present abusive relationships
4 · Stressful life events, bereavement, break-up of relationship
5 · Low self-esteem and disturbed self-image.

The therapist should begin to build up a profile of the client. Their background and early experiences are the foundations.

Treatment

Self-harm is a form of communication, taken up because the client is unable to express their thoughts or feelings in an adaptive manner. The therapist must ensure that the client retains the responsibility for their self-harm. As self-harm involves the client having control over an area of their life, maintaining control should be encouraged. The therapist must invest in providing the client with healthier alternatives to self-harming. In the short term, this usually creates a feeling of helplessness within the therapist. However, the long-term gain will be of great benefit to the client. They will not only keep the control, but will also be able to choose healthier ways of coping. Taking risks with the self-harmer is inevitable. However, the risks must be assessed, and the results of the risks reduced. A client who cuts 10 times a day may have been prevented from cutting 20 times a day. To allow the client to cut whenever they feel necessary may see episodes increasing to 30 times a day, as the client needs to gain control and accustom to the responsibility. Once this control is established, it is anticipated that the incidence of cutting will reduce.

The physical aspects of self-harming must be addressed. The client who cuts, burns or self-poisons should have the necessary skills to attend to their wounds and be able to access relevant medical care. The client retains control through the whole process of self-harming. As therapists, our instinct is to help. In the long term, this may prove to delay the client's progress.

In hospital settings, it is more accepted that harm reduction is more effective than prevention. For example, if a smoker who went into hospital smoking 10 cigarettes per day was to stop smoking, you would expect an increase in agitation, irritability, frustration and so on. Cutting, to a self-harmer, is an accepted part of their day, just as washing your face is to you. The progress that is to be made is about the self-harmers maintaining control and responsibility, and being willing to investigate avenues for healthier alternatives.

The therapist–client relationship should by now be one of trust and safety. The client should be encouraged to attend groups specifically for self-harmers. The client should have a good individual understanding of their self-harming, and will benefit from learning from others' experiences. Group work invariably allows the client to feel that they are not alone. The client will benefit from communicating with people who have experienced what they have experienced. Creative therapies – either individually or in a group setting – are becoming more acknowledged. The ability for clients to express themselves in the form of art, drama, music and the like is to be cultivated. Clients may prefer to keep a diary to express their feelings, and to monitor their progress to recovery.

It has also been suggested that help is more beneficial to the client at a time of crisis. The introduction of the Green Card that allows the client immediate access to a familiar health professional has reduced the need for prolonged in-patient stay (Morgan *et al* 1993). The client will feel a higher degree of safety just knowing that they have the card, and this psychological support, in many cases, may prevent crisis contact with mental health services. The distribution of the Green Card requires an individualised assessment to eliminate abuse.

Clients who self-harm represent a difficult and challenging group. The therapist's honesty and effective clinical skills will be trusty tools enabling them to carry out their task of making a difference.

Types of Depression

In this section, the different types of depression and the terminology used when describing clients' symptoms are explained. Diagnosis in psychiatry is a much debated issue, as there are positive and negative features of a diagnostic label.

Following an accurate assessment, a diagnosis will lead to an appropriate and rapid treatment plan, which can be followed by all health professionals. However, clients may present with differing symptoms but have the same diagnosis. Therefore, it is important to recognise the symptoms of the illness individually, and to treat the symptoms, as opposed to treating the diagnosis.

Mania

In a manic phase of illness, the client's mood becomes elated. Their usual social skills and inhibitions are diminished. This may result in them becoming over familiar and, in particular, sexually disinhibited. Their clothing and make-up will become much more colourful and revealing. Their perception of themselves alters and becomes grandiose: sometimes they believe they have excessive amounts of money, and then purchase items they can ill afford. Their speech content is significantly increased, and they exhibit flights of ideas where they move from one topic to another rapidly, with very little obvious connection.

They have a pronounced interest in the activities of those around them, and wish to involve themselves in interactions that may be inappropriate. Their sleep pattern is disturbed, and they may go for periods of up to a week with only a few hours sleep. Their dietary intake reduces, as they remain too preoccupied with their activity and the environment to concentrate enough to sit down and eat. This excessive motor activity may lead to physical neglect. Attempts to restrain this behaviour may result in the client becoming irritable, hostile and threatening.

Psychotic features may be present in manic episodes. Grandiose delusions are the most common, with the client having an over-inflated opinion of who they are and their abilities. Auditory hallucinations may also be present, with the voices reinforcing the grandiose nature of their delusions.

Manic episodes may result from psychological traumas. They can also occur in a client who may have recently experienced an episode of depression. Anti-depressant treatment and ECT may contribute to an episode of mania. Illicit drug use – in particular the use of amphetamines – frequently results in a manic episode.

Depressive episodes

Everyone, at times, has problems with lowering of their mood. This can be in connection with an occurrence in life that makes them sad, such as bereavement or the end of a relationship. Therefore, a diagnosis of a depressive episode should be made when depressive symptoms are present for a significant period of time – approximately three to four weeks – with the symptoms being present on a daily basis.

Low self-esteem and feelings of unworthiness are frequently present. These are usually accompanied by irrational anxiety concerning themselves and others around them. There are disturbances in sleep, and difficulties in getting to sleep. The client will lie there, ruminating over illogical thoughts and anxieties. Early morning wakening may be a feature of the symptoms. Dietary intake is affected, with the client displaying anorexia (a loss of appetite). They will usually complain of food having no taste, or having no motivation to eat. Motivation is invariably affected in episodes of depression. The client may be unable or unwilling to carry out everyday tasks. They see no point in undertaking these activities, or do not feel they have the energy to do these things. Cognitively, the client will frequently experience difficulties in their level of concentration. They may find it difficult to concentrate on simple tasks, or for periods of more than a few minutes. Their thinking is slow, and their thoughts are usually preoccupied. Conversation may be limited, and will require effective communication skills from the therapist to draw out information from the client. Clients will focus on their faults, and things that have gone wrong in their lives, and will express feelings of worthlessness.

Where depression alone is present, it is often referred to as a unipolar disorder. A bipolar disorder describes a condition where both depression and mania are present.

Seasonal affective disorder

The impact of the seasons, and variations in degrees of light has been a recognisable sign for many years, but it is only in the past 20 years that its serious effects have been acknowledged. Seasonal affective disorder (SAD) is an example of a major depressive disorder that can be affected by specific times of the year. As seasons change, our internal biological clocks change due to a variance in sunlight. The most frequent form of seasonal affective disorder occurs in autumn and winter, and the most difficult months are January and February.

Symptoms
- Lack of energy
- Excessive sleeping, in particular during the day

- Increased craving for sugary food and carbohydrates, usually resulting in weight gain
- Little interest in social activities
- Depression lifts in spring and summer

Estimates of the prevalence of seasonal affective disorder are between one and 10 per cent of community samples (Eagles *et al* 1999; Blazer *et al* 1998). The difference in the rates of prevalence is as a result of different ways of assessing the depressive symptoms and their seasonality. As the disorder is relatively rare, if the more rigorous definition is used, it can sometimes go undiagnosed for several years. The onset occurs in adolescence or early adulthood, and occurs more frequently in women than in men.

Causes

It is caused by increased levels of melatonin. This is a hormone whose levels are increased in periods when it is dark. During the winter months, there is decreased light exposure and therefore an increase of melatonin. This hormone is related to sleep, and therefore an increase in this may lead to an increase in lethargy.

Treatments

Phototherapy is the preferred choice of treatment, as it is effective and less invasive than drug treatment. Exposure to this artificial light should begin when symptoms first appear, and continue until the end of the problem season. Sufferers should aim to spend as much time as possible in the natural light within the winter months, using the light box to 'top up' their exposure. Unfortunately, for the treatment to be effective the client has to extend the length of the day by using the light in the morning from about 0600. Lengthening the day by using the light-box at the end of the day is less effective.

Phototherapy may prove to be ineffective as a treatment alone, and the client may require antidepressant medication.

Once seasonal affective disorder has been recognised, and an effective form of treatment acknowledged, the sufferer can work on a preventative plan of care prior to the winter months in order to prevent a relapse.

Postnatal depression

Following childbirth, many women experience changes in their mood, which are frequently referred to as 'baby blues'. This is a mild form of change, and is usually resolved within 72 hours of childbirth. During this period women may present with symptoms of anxiety, irritability, confusion, and periods of crying with little evidence of stimulus. These symptoms may be very different from the pre-morbid personality of the sufferer. Reassurance and support from health professionals and family usually help to resolve these symptoms. Postnatal or postpartum depression is diagnosed when these symptoms continue, and are still present six weeks after the birth.

Symptoms

- Loss of motivation
- Disturbed sleep patterns, not in relation to the baby
- Loss of appetite
- Feelings of worthlessness or hopelessness
- Thoughts of self-harm
- Feelings of detachment from the baby
- Concerns that they may not love their baby, or they might not love them
- Thoughts about harming the baby.

Approximately 12 to 15 per cent of women experience depression during the postpartum period (Hammen 1997). Diagnosis must follow an accurate assessment, as it may be easily missed. The demands of a new baby on the mother may result in changes in sleep pattern, and low levels of energy.

The cause is thought to be hormone level change during pregnancy and following childbirth. These hormone changes may produce chemical imbalances that in turn cause depression.

Risk factors

- Previous episodes of postnatal depression in other pregnancies
- Previous episodes of depression
- Stressful events around the time of the pregnancy, such as the death of a partner, the break-up of a relationship, or pregnancy as a result of rape or an abusive relationship
- Lack of social support, poor social environment, or low self-esteem are all predisposing factors.

Severe cases of postnatal depression are referred to as puerperal psychoses. These cases are extremely rare – approximately 0.1 per cent of the population (Hammen 1997). Women who suffer this will require in-patient treatment as they can experience delusions and hallucinations concerned with the death of the infant. The risk to the infant is often high, as the mothers may not believe that the child is theirs. They may think that it is an impostor, and see it as their duty to get rid of the child. Delusional thought content focuses on harm to the child or the mother.

Treatment

As with all types of depression, accurate assessment and relevant treatment are important. Antidepressant medication is prescribed in relation to the level of depression. Breast-feeding will result in the baby receiving the antidepressant in the breast milk, which may add to the mother's feeling of worthlessness, but must be weighed against all other relevant factors.

Health professionals must liaise to provide the most relevant support. GP, health visitor and mental healthworker have a responsibility to the mother and the baby during this difficult period. Community psychiatric nurses and health visitors should have a joint plan of care. Holden *et al* (1989) suggest that 'listening visits can be very therapeutic and health visitors' intervention during the early stages can be conducive to a good recovery.' However, the mental healthworker must assess when natural concerns become replaced by disordered thought processes.

In combined treatment, medication in the short-term is effective. However, cognitive therapy provides an opportunity to develop effective methods of dealing with problems.

Additional Reading

Blackburn IM & Davidson K, 1990, *Cognitive therapy for depression and anxiety: a practitioner's guide*, Blackwell Scientific, Oxford.

Blackburn IM & Davidson K, 1995, *Cognitive therapy for depression and anxiety*, Blackwell Scientific, Oxford.

Persons JB & Davidson J, 2000, *Essential Components of Cognitive Behaviour Therapy for Depression,* American Psychological Association.

Padesky C & Greenberger D, 1995, *A Clinician's Guide to Mind over Mood,* Guilford Press, New York.

Williams C, 2001, *Cognitive behaviour therapy for depression: a practical workbook*, Arnold, London.

Self-help Books

Burns D, 1998, *Feeling Good, the new mood therapy,* Avon Books, New York.

Fennel M, 1999, *Overcoming Low Self-esteem: A Self-help Guide Using Cognitive Behavioural Techniques,* Constable Robinson, London.

Greenberger D & Padesky C, 1996, *Mind over Mood,* Guilford Press, New York.

Gilbert P, 2000, *Overcoming Depression,* Constable Robinson, London.

Bagg C, 1978, *Answers to suicide,* Constable, London.

Beck AT, Ward CH, Mendelson M, Mock J & Erburgh J, 1961, 'An inventory for measuring depression', *Archives of General Psychiatry* 4, pp561–71.

Beck J, 1995, *Cognitive therapy: basics and beyond*, Guildford Press, New York.

Becker MH & Maimon LA, 1975, 'Socio-behavioural determinants of compliance with health and medical care recommendations', *Medical Care* 13, pp10–24.

Blackburn IM, Bishops GA, Whalley LJ & Christie JE, 1981, 'The efficacy of cognitive therapy in depression: a treatment trial using cognitive therapy and pharmaco-therapy, each alone and in combination', *British Journal of Psychiatry* 139, pp181–9.

Birchwood M, Spencer E & McGovern D, 2000, 'Schizophrenia: early warning signs', *Advances in Psychiatric Treatment* 6, pp93–101.

Blazer DG, Kessler RC & Swartz MS, 1998, 'Epidemiology of recurrent major and minor depression with a seasonal pattern. The national co-morbidity study', *British Journal of Psychiatry* 172, pp164–7.

Bowers WA, 1990, 'Treatment of depressed in-patients. Cognitive therapy plus medication, relaxation plus medication, and medication alone', *British Journal of Psychiatry* 156, pp73–8.

Bowlby J, 1953, *Childcare and the growth of love*, Penguin Books, London.

Bowlby J, 1982, *Loss sadness and depression*, Basic Books, New York.

Bowlby J, 1983, *Attachment*, Basic Books, New York.

British Medical Association and Royal Pharmaceutical Society of Great Britain, 2003, *British National Formulary*, British Medical Association and the Royal Pharmaceutical Society of Great Britain, London.

Brown GW, Davidson S, Harris T, Maclean U, Pollock S & Prudo R, 1977, 'Psychiatric disorder in London and South Uist', *Social Science and Medicine* 11, pp367–77.

Brown GW and Harris TO, 1978, *Social origins of depression: a study of psychiatric disorder in women,* Tavistock, London.

Brown GW, Adler Z & Bifulco A, 1988, 'Life events, difficulties and recovery from chronic depression', *British Journal of Psychiatry* 152, pp487–98.

Brown GW & Moran P, 1994, 'Clinical and psychosocial origins of chronic depressive episodes. 1. A community sample', *British Journal of Psychiatry* 165, pp447–56.

Brown GW, Harris TO & Hepworth C, 1995, 'Loss, humiliation and entrapment among women developing depression: a patient and non-patient comparison', *Psychological Medicine* 25, pp7–21.

Burns D, 1998, *Feeling Good: the new mood therapy*, Avon Books, New York.

Clark D, 1986, 'A cognitive approach to panic', *Behaviour Research and Therapy* 24, pp461–70.

Coppen A, 1967, 'The biochemistry of affective disorders', *British Journal of Psychiatry* 113, pp1237–64.

Cuijpers P, 1997, 'Bibliotherapy in unipolar depression: a meta-analysis', *Journal of Behavior Therapy and Experimental Psychiatry* 28, pp139–47.

Department of Health, 1999, *Safer service. National inquiry into suicide and homicide by people with mental illness report*, HMSO, London.

Dobson K, 1989, 'A Meta-analysis of the efficacy of cognitive therapy of depression', *Journal of Consulting and Clinical Psychology* 57, pp414–19.

Eagles JM, Wileman SM, Cameron IM, Howie FL, Lawton K, Gray DA, Andrew JE & Naji SA, 1999, 'Seasonal affective disorder among primary care attenders and a community sample in Aberdeen', *British Journal of Psychiatry* 175, pp472–5.

Fava GA, Rafenelli C, Grandi S, Conti S & Belluardo P, 1998, 'Prevention of recurrent depression with cognitive behaviour therapy: preliminary findings', *Archives of General Psychiatry* 55, pp816–20.

Favazza AR & Conterio K, 1989, 'Female habitual self mutilators', *Acta Psychiatrica Scandinavica* 79, pp283–9.

Freud S, 1917, *Mourning and Melancholia. Standard Edition,* Vol19, Hogarth Press, London.

Greenberger D & Padeskey C, 1995, *Mind over mood: change how you feel by changing the way you think,* Guildford, New York.

Hamilton M, 1960, 'A rating scale of depression', *Journal of Neurology Neurosurgery and Psychiatry* 23, pp56–61.

Hammen C, 1997, *Depression*, Psychology Press, Hove, England.

Harris TO, Brown GW & Robinson R, 1996, 'Befriending as an intervention for chronic depression among women in an inner-city', *British Journal of Psychiatry* 174, pp219–32.

Hawton K & Fagg J, 1988, 'Suicide, and other causes of death, following attempted suicide', *British Journal of Psychiatry,*152, pp359–66.

Holden JM, Sagovsky R & Cox JL, 1989, 'Counselling in a general practice setting: controlled study of health visitors' intervention in the treatment of postnatal depression', *British Medical Journal,* 298, pp223–6.

Hollon SD & Najavitis L, 1998, 'Review of empirical studies on cognitive therapy', in Frances AJ and Hales RE, *American Psychiatric Press Review of Psychiatry,* 7, pp643–66, American Psychiatric Press, Washington DC.

Jarrett RB, Schaffer M, McIntire D, Witt-Browder A, Kraft D & Risser R, 1999, 'Treatment of atypical depression with cognitive therapy or phenelzine: a double-blind, placebo controlled trial', *Archives of General Psychiatry,* 56, pp431–7.

Lam D & Wong G, 1997, 'Programmes, coping strategies, insight and social functioning in bipolar affective disorders', *Psychological Medicine*, 27, pp1091–100.

McGuffin P & Katz R, 1989, 'Genetics of depression and manic depressive disorder', *British Journal of Psychiatry* 155, pp294–304.

Morgan HG, Jones EM & Owen JH, 1993, 'Secondary prevention of non-fatal deliberate self-harm. The green card study'. *British Journal of Psychiatry* 163, pp111–12.

Morris R & Morris E, 2000, 'Contextual evaluation of social adversity in the management of depressive disorder', *Advances in Psychiatric Treatment* 6, pp423–31.

Murray R, Hill P & McGuffin P, 1997, *The essentials of postgraduate psychiatry*, Cambridge University Press, Cambridge.

Paykell ES, 1982, *Handbook of affective disorders,* Churchill Livingstone, London.

Rogers C, 1977, *On becoming a person: a therapist's view of psychotherapy*, Constable, London.

Ronalds C, Creed F, Stone K, Webb S & Tomenson B, 1997, 'Outcome of anxiety and depressive disorder in primary care', *British Journal of Psychiatry* 171, pp427–33.

Scott J, 1999, 'Cognitive and behavioural approaches to medication adherence', *Advances in psychiatric treatment* 5, pp338–47.

Scott J & Wright J, 1997, 'Cognitive therapy for severe mental disorders', *American Psychiatric Association Review of Psychiatry* 16, pp171–99.

Shildkraut JJ, 1965, 'The catecholamine hypothesis of affective disorders: a review of supporting evidence', *American Journal of Psychiatry* 113, pp509–22.

Schiedman EC, 1993, *Suicide as a psychache, a clinical approach to self-destructive behaviour*, Northvale, New Jersey.

Shaw BF & Segal ZV, 1988, 'Introduction to cognitive theory and therapy', in Francis AJ & Hales RE, *American Psychiatric Press Review of Psychiatry*, 7, pp538–53.

Smith J & Tarrier N, 1992, 'Prodromal symptoms in manic depressive psychosis', *Social Psychiatry and Psychiatric Epidemiology*, 27, pp245–8.

Stengal E, 1958, *Attempted suicide, its social significance and effects,* Oxford University Press, Oxford.

Thase ME & Wright JH, 1991, 'Cognitive therapy with depressed inpatients: An abridged treatment manual', *Behaviour Therapy*, 22 pp579–95.

Williams C, 2001, *Cognitive behaviour therapy for depression: a practical workbook,* Arnold, London.

Williams R & Morgan G, 1996, *Suicide prevention,* HMSO, London.

Wing J, Mann SA, Leff JP & Nixon JM, 1978, 'The concept of a case in psychiatric population surveys', *Psychological Medicine* 8, pp203–17.

Wright JH & Beck AT, 1983, 'Cognitive therapy of depression: theory and practice', *Hospital and Community Psychiatry,* pp1119–27.